MW01109106

MARRIAGE TO GOD BE THE GLORY,

MARRIAGE IS NOT A MAN THING, IT'S A GOD THING!

Carl Smith

Second Edition

iUniverse, Inc.
New York Bloomington

Marriage, To God Be The Glory
Marriage is Not a Man Thing, It's a God Thing!

iUniverse books may be ordered through booksellers or by contacting:

iUniverse
1663 Liberty Drive
Bloomington, IN 47403
www.iuniverse.com
1-800-Authors (1-800-288-4677)

ISBN: 978-0-595-52832-5 (pbk)
ISBN: 978-0-595-63590-0 (cloth)
ISBN: 978-0-595-62885-8 (ebk)

Printed in the United States of America

iUniverse rev. date: 2/17/2009

Introduction

Marriage Is Not A Man Thing, It's A God Thing!

Marriage was the first institution created by God for man. God knows what it is and how to make it work. God said it is not good that the man should be alone; I will make him a "helpmeet" for him. God then took from the Man, the sum total of Man and made a new creation; a "**woman**" a **"helper**" that was compatible with him. He knew exactly what he wanted her to look like and how she would appeal to the man. **She was like him in creation, yet different in purpose.** They were made to become perfect and walk with God. They were commanded to love one another, be fruitful, multiply and rule over the earth. **They were husband and wife! *Therefore, marriage is not a man thing; It's a God thing!*** Man did not create it, ***God created it, He ordained it and God recognizes only what he creates; that is the union between a man and a woman.*** A man shall leave his mother and father, and cleave to his wife and they shall be one flesh **(Genesis 2:24)**. Man shall not live by bread alone, But by every word that proceeds from the mouth of God **(Matthew 4:4). God spoke it, and so shall it be.**

The Importance of the Traditional Family

I remember when I was a child my brothers, sisters and I were so happy when our father came home from a hard days work. We would all gather around him, so happy that he was home. Mother would have his dinner prepared and he would sit and eat. We had already eaten and weren't hungry, however, whatever he would offer us we would eat because we loved him and he was our dad and we were so proud of him. He was kind, gentle and possessed a quiet and strong spirit. We knew that whatever the circumstances were, our father would protect and take care of us and when we were bad he would chastise us with love. We did not mind his chastisement because we knew that he loved us. We had the traditional family, a mother and father present in our home. **Today, the traditional family is being opted out by so-called alternative lifestyles, some voluntary and others by circumstances.** The traditional family is an ideal arrangement; however with so many divorces and changes of moral values and attitudes we are finding that divorce, incarceration, role reversals and other issues are diminishing the male role in marriage. Single parent homes are managed and cared for by women with children absent of the male influence, and men are assuming a single parent role in increasing numbers. **We are finding diminished discipline in the homes and that problem is spreading throughout society. Young girls are getting pregnant at an alarming rate and the boys are restless, full of testosterone with nowhere to go and nothing to do. They turn to girls and make them the objects**

of their affection not realizing that being a father is more than bringing a child into the world. They join gangs and get into trouble facing possible jail time. Girls are beginning to follow in their footsteps and are becoming increasingly bold toward their sexual orientation and desire for premature intimacy. In the absence of the traditional family those situations are greatly increased. The traditional family, regardless of its diminishing popularity, is greatly needed and warranted. **A two parent home, can greatly increase the survivability of the family, through promoting orderliness, stability, authority, development, pride, commitment and instilling moral values to their children.** The mother and father are the examples to follow, one plant and the other water and sometimes the roles can be reversed. However, under certain circumstances that is not always the case**. If the mother and father are both dysfunctional, then so is the family**. There are exceptions to the rule; some single parent homes have proven to be very good role models for others to follow. Women have proven to be very good at raising children alone, however, boys do need a father figure in their lives especially during their years as a teenager. There are situations and circumstances that a boy may face that his father can assist him with having experienced it himself. **A mother may teach her son how to be a good person, but a father should teach him how to be a man.**

> ***A mother may teach her son how to be a good person, but a father should teach him how to be a man.***

Of course there are no absolutes in this situation, certain circumstances may interfere with either process. People are human, no one is perfect. However, **the traditional family adds value to our society.** I learned how to be a man by observing my father's interactions with my mother, other men, employers and society as a whole. **He gave me a sense of pride in following his wisdom about life and circumstances that I may face. And I practiced what he preached (Deuteronomy 6:5-9).** My mother and I were very close as well; she was a virtuous woman who was the nucleus in our family. She taught us how to love one another, to be obedient and resourceful in our everyday lives. She helped us develop Christian values and led by example. **We attended Church regularly and were taught the importance of including God in our lives daily.** She and my father were inseparable, I enjoyed seeing the two of them interact with each other, and our family was happy and focused toward a common goal with love for each other and God being the fuel that sustained us. My mother and father are both deceased; however, they equipped me with values that have been with me since childhood. I am also in a traditional marriage and I enjoy it immensely! I look forward to spending quality time with my family on a daily basis. Sometimes we spend days apart because of my job, however, our love for each other is steadfast and wonderful. We are loving it!! . No family is perfect, there will be disagreements, the traditional family teaches you how to live and forgive. I believe the traditional family is here to stay; it is a gift from God and one of his Plans for mankind. **To God Be the Glory!**

Contents

To The Reader

This book will have a positive and profound effect upon your life and the way that you view the marriage covenant. It was written with "obedience to God in mind," and to follow his instructions for a lifelong marriage full of Spiritual Blessings, knowledge, wisdom, understanding and love. ***I recommend that you pray first then read the "7 keys to a successful marriage."*** *This will set in motion a foundation for you to build on for your marriage or marriage to be. Then start at the beginning. Refer to the book often to keep your marriage strong and vibrant. Remember to pray first.* **To God Be The Glory!**

What Is This Thing Called Marriage?

Marriage is a universal language. From the continent of Africa to the farthest regions of the world, people marry. No matter what religion, no matter what faith, marriage is a common language. Traditions differ, but its purpose is universal; two people join together for a life long commitment, have children and hopefully live happy forever. Whatever it's purpose or intent, man is failing this institution horribly. How can something so right, go so wrong? The simple answer **is Traditions, Attitudes and Beliefs**. The "Word of God" says that "marriage is honorable before the Lord and the bed undefiled" (Hebrews 13:4). **God's intent for marriage was not for the "Will of Man," but the "Will of God," it allows man to have pleasure in it while he fulfills Gods purpose. Marriage is the only institution where-in man can satisfy the flesh through intimacy without committing sin against God. Sex is exclusively for marriage.** Therefore, God has allowed us to indulge in the **natural** that becomes "**spiritual in union.**" He gave the command in the Garden of Eden to the newly married couple, whom He was, both Father and Mother of, He said to them, to be fruitful, multiply, replenish and subdue the earth (Genesis 1:28). God gave man dominion over every living creature that creeps upon the earth. He was made Master over all that lived, and Eve, his wife, was mother of all that lived. So then, what happened in the garden that caused man to lose it all? Let us begin with a definition of marriage. According to the bible, **Marriage is a permanent covenant or a union between a man and woman for the purpose of fulfilling the "Will of God."** According to the Bible, God said that it is not good that the man should be alone, I will make him a "helpmeet" for him. **Someone that is a "helpmeet" or "helper" for you means that they are in agreement with whom you are and what you are.** Therefore, Eve was a reflection of man with a different process of creation. She was created with a womb, hence woman. A man who finds a wife finds a good thing. He shall leave his father and mother and cleave to his wife and they shall become one flesh. **How do you become as one? By walking together in agreement. How can two walk together except they agree (Amos 3:3). When you become as one, you are in agreement, not in agreement as to every little problem that may arise, but in agreement as to The "Will Of God," What is God's will? "Gods Will" is for every being that he created to be or become a reflection of him through faith in him and obedience of his commandments.** God made man in his own image, when man committed sin against God he ceased being Gods image. In marriage you are to become what God intended for your marriage to be, that is blameless and without sin. When we disobey God, we are out of His "Will." The problem with many couples today, is that they do not understand what "Helpmeet" means; the wife may look at it as a form of slavery that has been instituted by man. Nothing is farther from the truth. **The Lord did not command the wife to be a slave to her husband, but to be under subjection to her husband in all things (Ephesians 5:24), this is the will of God that Glorifies Him, her obedience.** The devil caused disorder in the Garden of Eden by deceiving Eve to step out of "Gods Will." From the very beginning Eve was to freely subject herself to her husband Adam, but when she committed transgression against God, God made it the Law! (Genesis 3:16). Many women find it difficult to submit to their husbands; this is the enmity between the man and the woman. **For this reason, we must be born again, of the water (Word Of God) and of the Spirit (John 3:5). Marriage is a "Born Again Experience." Its very survival depends upon our renewing of Mind and Spirit.**

> ***Marriage is a "Born Again Experience." Its very survival depends upon our renewing of Mind and Spirit.***

Our walk with Christ is a Marriage Relationship, that relationship must also be with one another in our Marriage (Ephesians 5:22-33). **So then, marriage is an exclusive covenant between a man and a woman who chooses to**

join together in a type of matrimony. This covenant says to the world and everyone else around them that we are one in the sight of our God. The wedding ring is a symbol of that covenant and the vows made, saying, that they have chosen each other and are no longer available. Man had an adversary in the Garden whose intent was to put an end to man's authority and birthright. Satan saw the relationship between God and man and decided to attack the weaker vessel, the Lord says husbands be kind to your wives as unto the weaker vessel (1 Peter 3:7). Eve was not as knowledgeable as Adam about Gods creations or commandments. **The only attack on the institution of marriage is from Satan and those influenced by him. The bible says that he is the father of lies.** He introduced himself to the marriage through lies and deception. He first questioned the intellect of Eve, speaking through the serpent, Stating, yea, have God said ye shall not eat of every tree in the garden? Eve told Satan that God said we may eat of the trees of the garden, but we shall not eat of the **"Tree Of The Knowledge Of Good and Evil,"** for in that day we shall surely die. Satan then told her that God, who is the God of the universe, who created all things, was hiding the truth from them (Genesis 3:4). **Eve believed the enemy rather than God almighty. And in marriage, the first mistake that couples make is listening to the wrong people about their obedience to God. To the carnal minded this may sound like a fairy tale, but to children of God, it is the Gospel. This book is written for those who are willing to pattern their marriage according to the word of God, and is based on Scripture in the "King James Bible," I am writing the book as a guide for those who want to have a successful marriage based on the word of God. Adam had the sum total of all earthly knowledge, wisdom and understanding; he named everything on earth including his wife, Eve. Adam was a "Natural Man" and did not possess Godly wisdom; that was to come later. The natural man does not understand the Spiritual things of God;** this is the reason why he must be born again of the **"Water (Word Of God) and of the Spirit."**

The "Natural Man" (worldly) does not understand the Spiritual things of God. For this reason he must be "born again of the "Water (Word Of God) and of the Spirit."

Adam was a man who loved his wife and was willing to do anything to make her happy, including being disobedient to God. There are Adams present today in marriages, however, because they do not understand their wives and do not possess the Godly wisdom needed as leaders in their homes they fail God and their families. **A woman once asked the question; "Pastor," when should husbands listen to the advice of their wives? My response to her through guidance of the "Holy Spirit"** was that the bible tells man to love his wife as he loves himself. Jesus gave himself for the Church, referred to as his bride. So, **a man must love his wife as Christ loves the Church and listen to her whenever she is speaking the "Will Of God." How does a husband know when his wife is speaking the "Will Of God?" By dealing with her according to knowledge, knowledge of the word of God (1 Peter 3:7).** A man shall not live by bread alone, but by every word that preceded from the mouth of God; not only a knowledge of his wife, because man does not know another person's heart, only God knows the heart of a person. **When Sarah suggested to Abraham to go into her handmaiden Hagar to cause her to conceive, she was not speaking the "Will Of God;" God was to have Sarah to conceive, not her handmaiden. Abraham had no obligation to listen to her, but should have rebuked the suggestion,** however, he did as his wife suggested and fathered a child by Hagar whose name was ***Ishmael.*** Later, when Sarah had grown tired of Hagar masquerading around as the woman of the house because she bore Abraham a son, Sarah said to Abraham that Hagar and her son had to go, as Abraham began to speak, the Lord commanded him to listen to his wife! (Genesis 21:12) because Sarah was then speaking the **"Word And The Will Of God." A wife has great power in the things she says, as long as she is operating in the "Will Of God."** Sarah was right in what she said because she was the legitimate wife and was the woman to help carry out Gods promise to Abraham, see (Genesis 12:1-3). God had promised Abraham many blessings according Gods will and purpose along with Abraham's faith. **Believe God's promises for your marriage and have faith that you shall receive them.** Abraham could not believe that a man of his age **(99)** and a wife **just 10 years younger** could still bear children. **When you are married in Christ the impossible becomes possible.** Barren women have been known to conceive after prayer and supplication to the Lord. God tells us that we must love our wives as we love ourselves (Ephesians 5:28). **Too many men treat their wives like they are doormats, something to trample on. The only thing you should trample under your feet is the devil. Treat your wife with love, honor, respect and admiration. Be that pillar for her in difficult**

times. Let her know that you will never leave her or forsake her as Jesus promise to us.

> ***Too many men treat their wives like they are doormats, something to trample on. The only thing you should trample under your feet is the devil. Treat your wife with love, honor, respect and admiration. Be that pillar for her in difficult times. Let her know that you will never leave her or forsake her as Jesus promise to us.***

If separation becomes necessary, separate for a time, but then come back together. **Sometimes it just won't work, not all have returned back to Christ. Not every husband and wife will come back together**. Scripture speaks of divorce in certain circumstances. Some preachers preach that divorce is never an option, however, that is based upon their opinion rather than scripture. The Bible plainly tells us that sometimes divorce is necessary to free one from bondage. **Jesus told his disciples that if they were not willing to leave their mother, father, brother, sister, husband, or wife for his namesake they can be none of his disciples (Luke 14:26-27). This passage was to indicate that Jesus came first in their lives, and if need be the disciples must forsake all others who interfered in their walk with Christ. The bible also tells us that we are also married to another (Romans 7:4) and he is Jesus Christ.** Our walk with Christ must be absolute, the Lord tested Abraham by commanding Abraham to sacrifice his son Isaac; Abraham's obedience was proof of his love for God and Isaac's life was spared. Who do you put first in your life? If you profess to be a child of God; then without question, "Christ!" should be first in your life! **Some of you have husbands or wives who do not belong to you. And that is probably why there is no peace or trust in your home because you have destroyed someone else's.** In the marriage of David and BathSheba, David knew the only way to have her was if her husband Uriah was dead, David arranged for him to be killed in battle. Had Uriah died without David's intervention, the marriage between David and Bathsheba would have been honorable, for Gods word says "that if a woman's husband dies, (Christian woman) she is free to marry whomever she chooses," as long as he is a Christian. God is a forgiving God, so staying with that person is between you and your God. If you were divorced, what were the circumstances that lead to the divorce? What caused the marriage to be dissolved? Was it adultery, fornication or some other reason? Any of the above reasons can cause problems within a new marriage. **Not everyone will make it into heaven, and not all marriages will survive.** By staying in a bad marriage you may deny yourselves the opportunity to find a true, loving and compatible relationship chosen by God for you. Sure, marriages have ups and downs, always have hope; **but be sensible enough to know when the hope runs out and the end is inevitable.** Often-times the woman says, I want my independence, however, she shouldn't have married if she wants to live together but have separate lives. Gods Law says you shall become as one. **Coming together is not an overnight thing; there must be communication, commitment, understanding and forgiveness**. You can be different but you must still agree. That agreement must be in the Lord. That is what matters most. I constantly hear Christian women express their displeasure in not meeting a suitable Christian man for marriage. **The Lord says do not be unequally yoked with unbelievers, which narrow the field of potential husbands for the Christian woman.** Churches are full of women serving the Lord, but where are the men? **Christian women are being drawn too and seduced by ungodly men. No matter how fine looking or financially stable she think he is, she must not make that mistake. You are living two totally different lifestyles, one is holy and the other is unholy, they simply won't work. People are getting married for all the wrong reasons; looks, money, fame and fortune. All these add up to the three main things that destroy the soul. The lust of the flesh, lust of the eyes and pride of life.** In the "Garden Of Eden," Satan tempted Eve with all three, and she lost. She saw that the fruit was good for food, and that it was pleasant to the eyes, and a tree to be desired to make one wise. Eve was not satisfied with what God gave to her and her husband Adam, she wanted more. **We all want more, but when more is unhealthy and interferes with your relationship with God, then it becomes a curse and not a blessing. Do not allow the lust of material possessions to harm your**

relationship with Christ. Adam knew better, he knew that if he took the fruit it would bring a sentence of death upon himself, his wife and far reaching devastations upon the whole human race. **What you do in your marriage can have far-reaching consequences upon family generations to come.** Didn't Adam know that through disobedience he would bring the sentence of death upon all of mankind? Adam wanted to please his wife, Abraham wanted to please Sarah, **but pleasing God first should have been their top priority. It is not a sin to want to please your spouse, but it is a sin if you disobey God while doing so (1 Samuel 15:22).** The husband is ultimately responsible for what happens in the home. The Lord asked Adam, Adam, where art thou? He did not ask Eve, his wife. He ask the man, the leader of the family, and he is asking the same question today, where art thou? And men around the world will do exactly what Adam did; make an excuse for disobedience to Gods word. **The wife, however, can have a lasting effect upon the success of her marriage covenant by using a powerful tool to keep blessings coming into her home, that tool is Prayer. A praying wife is a powerful woman through her humbleness and chaste conversation (1 Peter 3:1-4).** Jesus said my "Father and I are One" and I do what my Father tells me to do. Jesus always glorified and honored the Father. The disciples called him "**Good Master.**" Jesus said the only one that is good is the Father. Jesus said Father, "I have done all what you said; now glorify me since the beginning of time." **"Jesus is the Glory of God" and the woman is the "Glory Of The Man" (1 Corinthians 11:7).**

> **"Jesus is the Glory of God" and the woman is the "Glory of The Man"(1 Corinthians 11:7)**

It does not make her any less than the man, but in order for her to be the glory of her "husband" she must first be obedient to God, then to her husband. The bible says wives be under subjection to your husband in all things (Ephesians 5:24). If she is not a Christian who loves and honor God almighty, she may find submission to her husband difficult, because she is carnal minded (worldly), and a

carnal minded person does not obey the word of God (Romans 8:7). What makes a woman desire to be submissive to her husband, are her love, faith and obedience to the word of God, and true love for her husband. Through my ministry I have experienced on occasion that non-Christian women can be true helpmeets to their husbands. If a woman understands her role in the family and abide by that role, she can be a good helpmeet to her husband. **To God Be The Glory**!

Getting Ready For Marriage

A woman may ask the question, why can't I find a good man that I would like to marry? First of all he must find her. But in order for him to find her, she must be mentally and spiritually ready for marriage. **There is a certain "manner of spirit" that causes a woman to respond to a man, verbally or non-verbally, "I am your wife, now come and claim me"(Genesis 24:1-67). Her spirit is ready to receive a husband. She is ready to be submissive, trustworthy, kind and possess a quiet and meek spirit. Some women may perceive these qualities as a weakness; however, a kind and meek spirit is a sign of inner strength, beauty and peace! A contentious spirit (quarrelsome) is never good for marriage! (Proverbs 21:19)(Proverbs 26:21).**

> ***A contentious Spirit (quarrelsome, argumentive) is never good for marriage! (Proverbs 21:19)(Proverbs 26:21)***

You are not married because you are not ready for marriage. As a wife, you must be willing to be submissive to your husband, follow him and accept his leadership. Manage a good clean home for him to rest **(Titus 2:5).** Be a good role model and teacher to children. Use knowledge, wisdom and understanding at all times and be willing to forsake all others for him. **If you are not willing to put him first in your life above relatives and friends, then you are not ready for marriage. This applies to him also; there is a certain spirit and time in a man's life that says, "I am your husband and I claim you as my wife," and your spirits must be in agreement (Genesis 29:15-30). His spirit is ready to receive a wife. He is kind, gentle, loving, giving, compassionate and possesses a strong inner peace. If children are involved, he accepts them as if he were their father; if he is willing to love and accept you, he is also willing to love and accept your children.** What are some good qualities that a man may possess that indicate he might be a good husband? Does he love and respect his mother? Does he display a genuine affection for you and your children, if any? Does he respect you? Does he have an education, a good job and transportation? Does he possess good humor? Does he have a passion for helping others? Does he give freely of himself and his time? **Does he have confidence in his abilities? Does he listen and be attentive to your needs?** Is he willing to try new and exciting things? Is he financially stable? Does he display direct eye contact when talking to you? These qualities are not absolute, but a foundation for a healthy relationship. **Look for other qualities that compliment him, such as living a true Christian life. The first step in marriage is to seek God first.**

> ***Look for other qualities that compliment him, such as living a true Christian life. The first step in marriage is to seek God first...***

Some people seek their mates first, then Christ. Can it still work? Yes, if you obey the laws of God, however, you can spare yourself a lot of pain by seeking God first. **The bible says unless the Lord builds the house they labor in vain that build it (Psalms 127:1).** First, go into prayer expressing the desires of your heart; don't be shy about it. **The Lord already knows what you want and if it lines up with His Will, you get it.** The Bible says God will give you the desires of your heart. Both men and women should express to God how and what they desire in a mate; looks, attitude, personality, spirit and whatever else you desire and you will be pleased with God's choosing, not yours. **Please be cautious, there are wolves among the sheep, and they will prey on you!** Take your time in your selection process; let God choose your mate for you, being overly anxious can cause you to choose someone that under different circumstances you would not have chosen. People sense when we are desperate. To some people being overly anxious will scare them away, to others; you may become a potential target for misuse and abuse. They see your actions as a sign of weakness. **The Bible says that the devil can also appear as an angel of light, for this reason, seek Christ first!** I know of a young woman who was in Christ and openly expressed that she was a virgin and was waiting for God to place a Christian man in her life for marriage. She allowed herself to be influenced by unbelievers and fell from grace. She could no longer express her claim, nor did she marry the non-Christian man. I grieved over her misfortune and went into prayer with her. **There are men and women in society today who have no intentions of marrying or getting married.** They will destroy your life if you are not careful; living a Christian life is far from them. Be alert to the wiles of the devil. **Fornication, shacking (unmarried couple living together), common-law marriage, same-sex marriages and marriage by deception (for money, fame etc.) are not ordained by God, and are of a sinful nature. Couples who have lived together without the sanctity of marriage will find they have very little excitement about it when or if they do marry.**

Couples who have lived together without the sanctity of marriage will find that they have very little excitement about it when or if they do marry.

Problems arise and many end up getting divorced, for there is nothing new or exciting to look forward too. The Lord says obey the "Laws Of The Land," and one law is that of living together as husband and wife is to obtain a "**Certificate of Marriage." Marriage is exciting, wonderful and an honor in the eyes of God! To God Be The Glory!**

7 Keys To A Successful Marriage

For every broken marriage is a successful one. **What distinguish one from the other are seven distinct characteristics that have proven to be most important in keeping your marriage vibrant and healthy.** We will briefly examine each on its own merits. The order of importance will appeal to each individual on a personal basis. The main idea is that all seven are of utmost importance. **Read them aloud to your marriage partner!**

Love

Respect

Praise

Honor

Trust

Prayer

&

Forgiveness

Love is considered the most important key, for without it our relationship or marriage is over before it begins. The Bible says that love hides a multitude of faults and **is the fulfillment of the law of God and that "God is love."** When we love our spouse we love ourselves and are attentive to their needs and desires above our own. "**I love you because you help complete me and fill my heart with joy. God put a special love in my heart for you, so that only he can love you more (Eph 5:25) (Tit 2:4).**"

Respect is gratitude and submissive to love. **To love me is to respect me.** Respect humbles the soul and allow love to flourish between you and me. Respect defines the importance of our relationship and set its parameters. **Without it, I can't love you the way that you deserve me to love you.** And I respect you because I love you **(Eph 5:33).**

Praise is endearing and pleasing to the soul. To praise means to admire you for who you are and what you are in my life. **I praise you because I love you and respect you. I praise you because you are wonderful and exciting to me.** I praise you because I have found you to be worthy. **(Eph 5:33).**

Honor- I stand before you to give you what is deserving of you. **I honor you because you have proven to be worthy and I find no fault in the way you treat me and satisfy our needs.** I honor you because I adore you. I honor you because God commands it. Your honor is my honor and because I honor you I also love you **(Rom 13:7) (1 Pet 3:7).**

Trust- The test of time and the transparency of your heart, soul and spirit have told me that **you are truly the love of my life here on earth.** You have captured my heart and done me no wrong. **When I am in your arms I feel safe and my love for you is like a fiery furnace.** You have allowed me to grow with you and never felt left behind. Because I trust you, I love you, respect you, praise you and honor you **(Prov 31:11) (Gen 39:4-9).**

Prayer- because we pray together our hearts are on one accord and **we realize that there is a higher power that keeps us and sustains us. God is foremost in our lives and in him all things are possible.** When we unite, we unite in love, peace and harmony with God and each other. **I love to pray with you, because praying bring us together better than anything else.** Look what God have done for us. Our needs are met. We are safe and we love each other, respect each other, praise each other, honor each other and trust each other. **Let's keep praying! (1Thes 5:17).**

Forgiveness- I forgive you because I love you and possess the 7 keys in my heart for you. **I too have faults and I am capable of making mistakes.** I know that you will forgive me to because you possess the same keys of marriage that I do. **God commands us to forgive one another (Mat 6:14-15) (Eph 4:32).** And because we pray often our hearts are full of love, forgiveness, and understanding. **I am glad that God chose you for me and me for you.** We are on one accord and I think God is pleased with us because we live by his **"Word"** and the seven keys. **To God Be The Glory!**

Why Won't He Marry Me?

There are many reasons why a man will not marry the woman he is supposed to love and be in love with. The truth is if he doesn't marry you after professing "undying love and devotion to you," he just "**doesn't love you enough**." It's not a matter of being in-love with you because both men and women can profess being in- love with their companions and not marry them. **It's just that they don't love you enough- to marry you.** You say, what do you mean, don't love me enough? **When you love someone "enough" that means you are willing to accept that person for whom he or she is and include that person in your life "unconditionally for the rest of your life." Unconditional love presents special challenges of the heart because you face the unknown and uncertain conditions that you promise to deal with in your heart unconditionally**. What if you find out that your spouse is hiding something from you, that if you had known before marriage you may not have married her because of it; a terminal illness, a handicap or other situation that may be detrimental to your marriage. **Men, especially fear that thing called "commitment" because they are afraid that they may not be able to live up to your expectations or theirs; or he is basically into himself and is selfish about his love. Marriage is an unselfish act of love.** Children, finances, relatives, other commitments and even the appearance, personality and attitude of the woman he loves can be a turnoff to a man who considers these things of utmost importance.

"Women are also increasingly avoiding or delaying altogether the sanctity of marriage, preferring an alternative lifestyle rather than a more traditional monogamous relationship." They themselves are shunning marriage for fear of the responsibility that goes along with it. Marriage is a full time occupation and you must be equipped spiritually, mentally, physically and emotionally to deal with it! In today's world the majority of men and women are not prepared for marriage. There is no "free pie in the sky," marriage is work and if you are not willing to work for it, then you should stay out of it! There are many single parent households today. Some men and women simply will not get involved or marry a person with children. If children are involved, mention them in the course of your conversation. **Do not assume that the person is not interested if they are unresponsive**. Give them enough time to consider if they should continue in the relationship, after all, taking on an immediate family presents many challenges that some people are not willing to commit to. **Good communication is the key to knowing the unknown.** For the woman, Good communication can find out what he likes and dislikes. Join him whenever possible in considering those things that may be good for the relationship. Go out on several dates before introducing your children to him. This may give you time to decide if you want to continue seeing him. You may spare your children a minor disappointment. **A meek and humble spirit is loved and appreciated by most men. Forget about the feminist movement, it should be against things other than the man you love or desire to marry.** A little assertiveness adds spice to the relationship. Use it with wisdom! **What is the key element that makes a man want to marry a woman? TRUST! If a man can trust a woman he can love her, and if he can love her, he will marry her. Love and trust of "spirit" is the key element that makes a man want to marry a woman.**

> ***Love and Trust of "spirit" is the key elements that makes a man want to marry a woman.***

If a man have doubt in his heart about the woman in his life, there is doubt that he will marry her, remove the doubt! Can he trust her with his heart, his fragile ego? What about his friends, if a man leaves his home to travel the world over, he would like to have the assurance that the woman he left would love him the same way when he returns. Can the same apply to the woman? Yes! Can she trust him with her heart, can she trust him to protect her, to provide a good home for her and children, if any; will he assure her that he will never leave her? Why are there so many problems in male and female relationships? **The main problems are communication and understanding. Communication is the key to finding out if you are compatible in a relationship and understanding is a major key to sustaining it. True love is not dominating, or intimidating (1 Corinthians 13:1-8).** Sometimes, regardless of what good things we bring to a relationship, it just doesn't work, some people refuse to change or do things differently to make the relationship work! Don't fault yourself, **water and oil does not mix and you can't change that, if the love is not there in your relationship, cut your losses before you get married and move on!** My wife Gloria and I had no hesitation about our love and commitment to one another. We knew that our marriage was from God. **Women who have lived an independent lifestyle without a male companion may find it a difficult challenge to honor the words "submit to her husband."** Be patient, if your relationship is of God and you understand His purpose for your marriage, it will work. **It is a wonderful feeling when you know that God chose your mate for you. He doesn't make mistakes; with him involved in your marriage, you will succeed in good times and bad. Evil may attack your marriage, but God gives the protection through his "Holy Spirit" to overcome it.** Remember, marriage is honorable before the Lord and the bed is undefiled. **To God Be The Glory**!

The Blood Covenant

The act of marriage is intended to be a blood covenant between the man and his bride, and should be permanent and binding. **The hymen is a type of veil that is to be broken only by the bride's husband. The blood covenant is then established. This is the most precious gift a bride can give to her husband during their wedding consummation; her virginity.** However, because so many boys and young girls start sex at a very early age that blood covenant is between children who cannot understand the value, honor and ordination of a true and loving marriage.

> ***That "Blood Covenant" is between children who do not understand the Value, Honor and Ordination of a true and Loving Marriage***

Therefore the majority of young women today cannot establish a blood covenant with their husbands because they lose their virginity at such a young and tender age. **Virginity is a great honor for a young bride and was highly esteemed from the beginning of mankind.** Parents must instill within their children the importance of sexual abstinence before marriage at an early age and the establishment of a holy covenant with a perspective marriage partner. Parents should help their children achieve a spiritual foundation in Christ. Without it, it will be difficult to maintain abstinence. **When our daughters remain virgins until marriage so will our sons, because they will have no choice. Peer pressure will be a thing of the past, just say no!!** This in itself will be a blessing for the entire human race. Sexually transmitted diseases will be greatly reduced, the number of illegitimate children will drop considerably and abortion clinics will all but close. **Unwanted pregnancies will be drastically reduced all because of the words and actions of "Abstinence Until Marriage." Abstinence can be achieved by the surrendering of one's life to Christ. Thank God for Jesus, because with Christ, he will strengthen and sustain you until marriage. "Through Christ I was able to remain celibate for 7 years before I met and married Gloria. Without Christ in my life, it would not have been possible."**

"Through Christ I was able to remain celibate for 7 years before I met and married Gloria. Without Christ in my life, it would not have been possible."

A young man and woman may have sex before marriage and can no longer be considered virgins in the consecration of marriage, as Christians **they are born again of the "Water and of the Spirit."** Therefore, their spirit is renewed, although she can never replace her hymen, or become a virgin again. **But she and her husband can become "virgins in spirit," thereby making the marriage a holy, binding and permanent covenant, because of the blood of Jesus, which he shed for us that we may live. To God be the Glory!**

After Sex Then What

The lustful craving of the flesh can be uncontrollable. **The Bible tells us that the spirit is willing, but the flesh is weak (Matthew 26:41).** People find themselves in bedrooms of strangers that they hardly know just to satisfy the cravings of the flesh. They blame their husbands, wives, too much alcohol, drugs or some other reason for inappropriate behavior. Or they like the conversation and the way the person looks. Once the sexual act is over, they find they have very little in common. Sometimes the relationship blossoms into something meaningful and other times it's a disaster. As a result, unwanted pregnancies and children are brought into the world, sexually transmitted diseases are introduced and are sometimes fatal. Relationships are broken, and many children are abandoned and left without the father's presence in the home. **Sex must never be a basis for a relationship, but an addition to the outward expression of love for one another. A woman should never give freely of herself through intimacy without the sanctity and benefits of marriage.**

A woman should never give freely of herself through intimacy without the sanctity and benefits of marriage.

Her body is the "Temple Of God" (1 Corinthians 3:16); and must not be defiled. Fornication, homosexuality and adultery destroys the tradition of marriage and eliminates the "blood covenant." If a jeweler offers a man a precious stone to use as he chooses, why should he pay for it! Easy come easy go. You are that precious stone. Young girls and women are giving of themselves that precious gift from God freely to undeserving boys and men, who use their bodies for sexual gratification and no real commitment to them. What a tragic mistake! If you don't think that your body is precious and a "Sacred Temple of God," neither does he! Ladies, stop the cycle of misuse and abuse of the 'Temple Of God," which is your body. Men and women alike should commit themselves to abstinence until marriage. The Lord gave the first husband and wife a commandment to be fruitful, multiply and replenish the earth. The command was given only after they were married **because in the law of God, sex is only permitted between a man and woman after a marriage covenant has been established.** Worldly lust is present throughout society, homosexuality, fornication and adultery is more accepted and allowed. Those who oppose these acts of lustful disobedience are criticized to the point that they retreat in an aire of confusion and made to feel guilty for their moral and Christian beliefs. **There is nothing to be ashamed of when you are living a chaste and Holy life! The Lord tells us that those who practice immoral sexual acts (Romans 1:26,27,28) will not enter into the kingdom of God (1 Corinthians 6:9). To God Be The Glory!**

Marriage Is Not A Man Thing, It's A God Thing!

Marriage was the first institution created by God for man. God knows what it is and how to make it work. **When he made woman he made her the most beautiful, magnificent and intelligent creation for man**. He knew exactly what he wanted her to look like and how she would appeal to the man. **Therefore, Marriage is not a man thing; it's a God thing! And man must live it according to the "Laws Of God" in order for it to survive! Man did not create it, God did, and he only recognizes what he creates. He knows what it is and what it's for, and that is a binding covenant between a man and a woman. He sanctified and ordained it. "A man shall leave his mother and father and cleave to his wife and they shall be one flesh" (Genesis 2:24). Man shall not live by bread alone, but by every word that proceeded out of the mouth of God (Matt 4:4). God spoke it and so shall it be.** The Lord says, "I will make him a helpmeet (woman, wife) for him, and they shall be fruitful and multiply." **It's not about man; it's about God and his Glory. Therefore, marriage must be Holy before him. Marriage is not just between the man and the woman, but God must be involved in our marriages. He is our source of strength and comfort during difficult times. He restores order and peace in our homes through the Holy Spirit.**

God must be involved in our marriages. He is our source of strength and comfort during difficult times. He restores order and peace in our homes through the Holy Spirit.

Satan comes but to steal, kill and destroy your marriage. Steal the joy from your marriage; kill your love and passion for one another by sowing discard among you. **What two God put together let not man put asunder (Matthew 19:6). That is why it is so important to seek Him first, and all other things will be added on to you.** God gave man two greatest commandments: love Him first and to love your neighbor as you love yourself. **It's about love, Godly love; only Godly love for your spouse will survive, only Godly love can forgive. Love hides a multitude of sins.** When we argue, we get angry, God says be angry, but do not sin. **We sin when we harbor anger, hate, resentment and revenge in our hearts.** If the husband is caught cheating, the wife out of hurt, anger, betrayal and resentment may go and do likewise. This in itself is a horrible travesty. It only helps to destroy an already broken relationship. **So, what is the answer? Prayer, Fasting and Christian counseling.** You may separate for a while to heal your heart and spend time in prayer with the Lord, who has all the answers, read **John 8:3-11; on an act of judgment and forgiveness.** The woman wasn't the only guilty party, was she? Somewhere in your relationship, your spouse had to forgive you for something you did, probably without your ever knowing that you caused the pain. **Keep the "I AM" (God) in your marriage and he will keep the "I DO" in your hearts. Honey, I do love you, I do honor you, I do respect you, I do try to understand you, and I do need you: These "I DO'S" are so important in a marriage. Write them on the tablets of your heart. Remember why you married and the wonderful things that attracted you to each other.** Change or leave your surroundings for a while. Spend quality time in your Marriage. Remember; **marriage is an investment, you get out of it, what you put into it! To God Be The Glory!**

I'm The Man! Oh Really...

Our churches are full of women and children, but where are the men? God has commanded men to be leaders in their homes; however, in most examples the wife becomes the more spiritual and vocal leader. It wasn't designed that way. The husband and wife roles are clearly defined in the Bible; however, God equipped her in a way that if the need arise she can temporarily maintain the home. If the husband falls to an illness, or finds himself no longer the major breadwinner, the wife can take over the affairs of their home. **Regardless of her financial status or position in life, the husband is still the leader in the home. The Bible says that there is neither male nor female, we are all one in Christ Jesus (Galatians 3:28); however, the husband is the head of the wife, this is his God given and appointed position in his home (Ephesians 5:23).**

> ***The husband is the head of the wife, this is his God given and Appointed position in his home (Ephesians 5:23)***

The wife cannot take it away; neither can he take away her role. Although he may temporarily assume her role from time to time, he cannot replace her. Through my Ministry, I find that men are neglecting their true responsibility in the home and attempts to pass it on to the wife until a more convenient time for him to reassume it. **He plays the role of "I'm the man" Monday through Saturday, and disappears on Sunday, the very day that his leadership is so greatly needed in his home. My wife Gloria never demands anything from me, but she expects me to be the man God made me to be; and she helps me to become that man. She loves me, she honors me, she submits to my leadership, she adores me and desires me. She is my friend, my lover, and my wife.** Men from all walks of life can glorify God by setting examples for their children in the ways of true Godly worship. **It is extremely important to be a source of spiritual guidance and information in his home.** So then, why aren't more men in the Church? The truth of the matter is, that leadership in the Church have not been kind to men, and there have certainly been more negatives than positives, and of course sometimes it's warranted**, but for the most part men need to be honored and recognized when they play a key role in their families development and in the neighborhood in which they live.**

> ***But for the most part, men should to be honored and recognized when they play a key role in their family's development and the neighborhood in which they live.***

Many wives are guilty of the "**under the authority of the Pastor**" syndrome. They mistakenly place a Pastor as their headship and not their husband. Let me set the record straight**; the Pastor is the leader of the congregation in your church. The Pastor is not your head, your husband is (Ephesians 5:22-24), and Christ is the head of your husband. Many wives ignore the wishes of their husbands and submit to the instructions of their Pastors over that of their husbands. This of course causes a conflict and place a strain on the relationship with her husband.** Husbands stress the displeasure with their wives that they don't practice true biblical principles. They shout Praise the Lord! in morning church services and ignore the duties of a wife in the evening. "**No other man should be given privileges equal**

to or above that of your husband." This in itself drives away many men from the church and creates a "diminished role of leadership" in his home for lack of biblical knowledge. We cannot accept one part of the bible and reject that which is not favorable to our desires. For this reason it is extremely important to develop understanding and obedience to the word of God, regardless of whether we agree with it or not. Christian women must marry a Christian man, and vice versa. The unbelieving spouse can cause a serious problem with your salvation. **The Bible says be obedient to those who have rule over you. The husband have rule over the wife, what makes it difficult is the wife's attitude toward her husband's authority and how he conducts himself in the exercise of that rule. Blessed is the home that has order in Christ! To God Be The Glory!**

Reinventing Me

Throughout our lives we make changes to better our lives our surroundings or conditions we live in. It becomes a habit that we find hard to break. So, when we marry we try to change or mold that person into what we think they should or ought to be. **A word of caution: Don't Try To Change Your Spouse; you married the person for whom he or she is. And now you want to change him.** By attempting to change your spouse, you're stirring up a nest of anger, disappointment and resentment. **Examine yourself first! You may find that it is you and not your spouse that are in need of change!** When we try to change others, we are in fact saying that we are displeased with something in their lives, or they are doing things that we disapprove of, whether that thing is good or bad. **Of course, unacceptable behavior is a necessary change! And a course of action should be taken to eliminate it.** Sometimes it can be a good thing that we disapprove of. If your spouse is a cheerful giver, you may feel that people are taking advantage of him and want him to be more cautious. However, that act of kindness will prove to be more of a blessing to your family, because the Bible says that God loves a cheerful giver (2nd Corinthians 9:7). A desire to want to change someone comes from three things that the Bible warns us about, **the lust of the flesh, lust of the eyes and pride of life.** The thing that attracted you to your spouse is now something that you no longer desire, the novelty has worn off. Perhaps your wife have gained a few pounds, this is especially true with women who are bearing children. The husband no longer finds her extra weight appealing. Her concern about her weight and the husband's displeasure places a strain on their marriage. A spouse that smokes may cause an undue hardship on the marriage, especially when their spouse is allergic to cigarette smoke. Maybe a spouse is a heavy drinker, a drug user, a womanizer, or adulterer. All these situations bring about a desire to change someone or something. **It is not your responsibility to change your spouse. Change comes from an inward conviction, caring heart and lots of love!**

It is not your responsibility to change your spouse. Change comes from an inward conviction, caring heart and lots of love!

That conviction must come through the word of God. The caring heart must come from a desire to please God in all that we do, and the love must come from the Spirit that God has instilled within us; the "HOLY SPIRIT." Loving someone is allowing that person to be all that God has created them to be; interfering in their lives mean you are interfering with God's creation and plan for that person. If you want someone to change something that is bad or destructive in their lives, introduce them with loving kindness to the word of God. **Leave change up to God. To God Be The Glory!**

The Point of No Return

There is life and death in the power of the tongue. We as humans are very fragile because of the words we speak. **Remember, *"and God said,"(Genesis 1:1-24) he spoke the word and it was so*, so is it in your marriage. You have the Power of, "*and she said, and he said.*"** The very words you speak can bring life or death to your marriage. **When we are talking to people, we want them to understand what we are saying and the meaning behind it. We can speak blessings or curses upon one another. The spoken word is what establishes us. "*In The Beginning Was The Word,*" and communication of that word is what *sustains us: And God said, let there be light (Genesis 1:3)*.**

> ***The spoken word is what establishes us. "In The Beginning Was The Word, "and "Communication of that Word" Is What Sustains Us: And God said, let there be light (Genesis 1:3).***

It is extremely important to say those things that do not leave a negative lasting impression upon the person to whom you spoke. There is a point in everyone's life wherein if that point is reached; there is no longer a chance for compromise. **A husband or wife can reach the "Point Of No Return" by what they say and do to each other.**

For some people, rude, vulgar and demeaning language can destroy a relationship. Physical and or emotional abuse, incest, homosexuality, lesbianism, drunkenness, lies and even temporary abandonment may prove to be fatal to an already fragile relationship. **A husband, who abuses his wife frequently, only to apologize and repeat the act over and over again, may not realize that he is getting to the "Point Of No Return" with her. There are no more excuses or apologies accepted, for there is pain in her heart and her love begins to fade, for now she knows that it is over, but he doesn't. The love that she cherished for him so deeply has been destroyed by his selfish abuse of her heart. No one knows the heart of a person except God and that person. Men are notorious for misunderstanding nonverbal cues from their wives. He continues on his quest daily as if blinded by her kindness and outward affection toward him, wishing that for once, he would recognize her as a true, loving and faithful partner in their relationship.** Women often benefit from the love, respect and adoration that her husband gives her by sometimes using sex, food and affection as key weapons to get him to give her what she wants. Men further fuel the fire by using certain terms as "I'm in the dog house," meaning that his wife controls where he sleeps and commands him to obey. **A Christian marriage must be based on sound doctrine. The Lord commands us not to let the sun go down on our wrath (Ephesians 4:26).** The couple should come to an agreement and or compromise, respecting each other's wishes before retiring for the evening. How often have we heard a widower say, "I never got a chance to tell her that I'm sorry." **Marriage should never consist of anger, hate, jealousy, envy, lies, adultery or fornication; but love, honor, respect, joy, peace, compassion, understanding, humbleness, kindness, empathy, meekness and any other positive attributes to add to a successful marriage. But, what about forgiveness?** The Lord commands us to forgive one another. **However, he did not command a man or woman to stay in a continuously violent and emotionally abusive relationship. You forgive them and go on with your life someplace else!**

However, he did not command a man or woman to stay in a continuously violent and emotionally abusive relationship. You forgive them and move on with your life someplace else!

Some people base their marriage upon it being a ticket to heaven. Not so, **your marriage whether good or bad will not get you into Heaven because there are no marriages in heaven (Matt 22:30).** ***It is what's in your heart, having faith, obedience and the love of God that gets you there.*** Be careful when you argue or have disagreements, **Satan is listening and God is watching. To God Be The Glory!**

Controlling Anger and Preventing Abuse

In our marriages we face many challenges ahead of us. Some people handle those challenges easier than others. **Some people look at their spouse as an object of their frustration and there the cycle of anger and abuse is born. That abuse can be physical, verbal or both.** When we become frustrated we must not forget that **our frustration is an individual thing regardless of what or who caused it.** People in our lives can either add to it or help to diminish it. **A key consideration is communication and self-control. Consider the consequences of your actions (Ephesians 4:26-27).**

> ***When we become frustrated we must not forget that our frustration is an individual thing regardless of what or who caused it. A key consideration is communication and self-control. Consider the consequences of your actions (Ephesians 4:26-27)***

A kind word turns away wrath (Proverbs 15:1). Remember, nothing is impossible in Christ Jesus. With man, yes, but in Christ all things are possible (Ecclesiastes 3:1). The Bible tells us that there is a season and time for every purpose under Heaven. **We will at some time in our lives, face challenges that will test our resolve.** And depending upon our lifestyle, our faith, our relationship with Christ, and our relationship with our spouse will determine how we handle those challenges and whether we will succeed or fail. **There are no failures in Christ Jesus.** We may lose our money, our homes, our jobs, but in Christ we have the victory. **Your spouse is your equal, not your child. Do not diminish his or her position in your marriage simply because you're angry or frustrated. When we get angry, we say things that are meant to hurt embarrass, control, intimidate or correct what we perceive as actions unfavorable to our lives or well being (Ecclesiastes 7:9).** ***Our actions can cause tremendous harm to the person we say we love, honor and cherish.*** **Do not attempt to control or discipline your spouse!** We must always consider their feelings and the effect of our actions in their lives. She loves you, he loves you, and they are placed in our lives to help bring us peace, love, comfort and companionship. **Always deal with your spouse in the "Spirit of the Matter."** Will we harm ourselves? Will we say things that are demeaning and abusive about ourselves? The Bible says no man hated his own flesh --. You are one with your spouse. **When he hurts, you hurt. When she is full of joy, so should you be. Share each other's joy and pain alike. This builds a strong and enduring marriage, To God Be The Glory! Get excited about-facing your challenges of the day; invite recommendations, suggestions and anything else from your spouse that may help in solving the object of your frustration. If that object is your spouse, approach her with love and respect, always considering the enduring love that you are building upon.** Look at your spouse with optimism and invite God into your relationship through prayer and fasting. **Come together and agree on a course of action.** Remember Christ said that **where two or three are joined together in his name, He is there in the midst of them (Matthew 18:20). He will never leave you or forsake you. When you feel like shouting at your spouse, give her a hug. When you feel like criticizing, give him a compliment. When you feel like frowning, give her a loving smile. Never, ever, strike the person you love!!**

When you feel like shouting at your spouse, give her a hug. When you feel like criticizing, give him a compliment. When you feel like frowning give her a loving smile. Never, ever strike the person you love!!

If ever you desire to do so, your relationship is in harm's way and you should seek Christian counseling immediately. **Striking your spouse is a "slave owner mentality" and must be immediately dealt with and abolished.** The Bible says that weeping may endure for a night, but joy cometh in the morning **(Psalm 30:5). During times of trials and tribulations in our lives, open the lines of communication, and make your intentions clear. Invite suggestions and feedback, put yesterday behind you and work on the day at hand. Place those problems you cannot solve in God's hands. Worry doesn't solve problems; love, prayers, faith, obedience and action solve problems. Always remember to say, "I love you." To God Be the Glory!**

The Ultimate Betrayal

You've been hurt, your spouse committed adultery, what do you do? **First forgive, yes forgive (Matthew 6:14-15). Sometimes it is hard to forgive someone who has betrayed your trust, but forgiveness is the first process of healing (Mark 11:25,26) (Luke 17:3,4).**

> ***Sometimes it is hard to forgive someone who has betrayed your trust, but forgiveness is the first process of healing (Mark 11:25,26)(Luke 17:3,4)***

Anger, resentment, envy, and revenge are things that God does not want in your heart and you must remove them in order for Him to act on your situation. It takes time for healing of the heart. **The Lord says be angry and sin not (Ephesians 4:26); do not recompense evil for evil. The next thing is to go into prayer and fasting.** Accept help from love ones that are in Christ; however, do not be influenced by opinions. Base your decisions upon the "**Word of God.**" Your relationship may not be healed, but you will be. You may decide to move on; however, **do not be anxious in starting a new relationship. Give yourself time to heal completely.** Sometimes emotional scars run deep, depending upon the level of love and commitment you had in your marriage. **How will you know when you are healed? When you are able to laugh with the person who betrayed you and have no animosity toward that person, only Godly love and peace in your heart. Believe me, it is a wonderful feeling to be able to do that with someone who betrayed you. You see, God is love, and when you show love, you show the God in you. Evil cannot stay where there is love**! What caused the selfish act of adultery? First of all; **adultery is not an option.** It doesn't matter how troubled your marriage is, how lonely you get, how intimately deprived you feel, **adultery is not the answer. So, what is the answer? Seek ye first the Kingdom Of God and his righteousness and all these things shall be added onto you"(Matthew 6:33).** Did you seek Him first, and then seek your mate? **The Lord will give you the desires of your heart, but you must desire to serve Him first! And that desire** must be in agreement with "**His Will and Purpose"** for your life. Marriage should never be a selfish act, but in accordance with the "Will Of God." **Communication is the second thing in a fragile relationship. You cannot solve the problem without communication.** Define your problem, and then devise a solution to solve it. Be optimistic in your approach; pray for knowledge, wisdom and understanding first. You will be amazed at how wonderful God will deal with your situation. **To God Be The Glory!**

What To Do When You Are The Betrayer

Sometimes in your life you may be tempted to betray the one you love. The Bible says that the "**spirit is willing but the flesh is weak" (Matthew 26:41) and we are drawn away by our own temptations (James 1:14).** Your temptation can prove your faithfulness, Love for God, and your love for your spouse. How much do you love her? **How committed are you to your marriage? (Ephesians 5, 25, 28).** Do you allow things, situations or people to tear down the strength of your relationship? Before this happens, you will see warning signs, such as a decrease in communication, disinterest in your spouse, physical and or emotional abuse. Quick outburst of anger for things that are trivial or unimportant. Lying about your whereabouts, losing interest in intimate moments with your spouse or having a hurry-up and finish attitude. **When you see these warning signs take inventory of yourself first. Many times we look at our spouse as the reason for our unfaithful behavior, however, the spouse may contribute, but you are the ultimate reason. There is no situation in your marriage so grave that it gives you a reason to cheat on your spouse**!

There is no situation in your marriage so grave that it gives you a reason to cheat on your spouse!

The key to being and remaining faithful to your spouse is deep abiding love; trust, faith and respect for your marriage. Love for God, and love for your children, if any. Trust is secondary, admiration is third, Respect is forth and commitment is number five. You must "**love God first**" in order to show Godly love for your spouse. You "**must trust the spirit**" of the one you love to feel safe and secure in your marriage. You "**must possess a deep admiration**" for her because she is the most beautiful, wonderful and exciting woman in your life. You must "**respect your spouse**" for who he or she is and by being appreciative for the things she does with you, for you and to you. **And finally, commitment; you must possess the first four in order to possess number five.** ***Without love there is no commitment, without trust there is no commitment, without admiration there is no commitment. Without respect there is no commitment. To be committed means all five encompass your whole being.*** **The first thing to do after you have betrayed your spouse is to pray. Go into prayer and repent to God first. Then go to your spouse with a heart that is seeking forgiveness and true sorrow for your unfaithfulness. Then seek Christian marital counseling. On occasion some people have no regrets for their unfaithfulness. What if you are not sorry for your infidelities and decide not to participate in counseling. The bible says that Moses gave a "certificate of divorce" because of the hardness of man's heart. Don't allow a cold unloving heart to destroy your marriage, if that is the case, end the relationship and move on; your spouse deserves better! To God Be The Glory!**

Staying Together

Your trust have been broken, you are angry, upset and trying to make sense of what has happened to your marriage. You began to wonder "Am I at fault, what did I do wrong to deserve this"? The pain can bring about resentment, revenge, hate, remorse and sometimes things unimaginable. This is a time for you to dig inside of yourself in the **"Spirit of the Matter"** and ask God for strength. Do not try to go it alone! Confide in a good friend or relative who loves you and care about your well being. **Sometimes, regardless of how well we treat someone or what we do for that person, it may go unappreciated. Jesus gave his life so that all may live, he did not receive that love back in return, however, he loved us anyway.** First of all, realize that both of you need healing; you and the one who betrayed you. His healing must come from the realization that he needs help and to seek Christian counseling. **Your healing must come from your faith, obedience and trust in the "Word Of God;" that he will see you through your situation**. Put the past behind you, The Lord put your past behind him. Do the same for your spouse. You made the decision to stay, "**now deal with it**" without revenge, or remorse. **Have confidence that your marriage will thrive and make it happen. Always be aware of those things in your surroundings that may hamper, threaten or destroy your marriage and deal with them according to knowledge of the "WORD Of GOD". Never allow an outside influence to cause**

separation between you and your spouse; you must walk together in agreement. A House Divided Will Not Stand (Mark 3:25).

> ***Never allow an outside influence to cause separation between you and your spouse, you must walk together in agreement . A House Divided Will Not Stand (Mark 3:25)***

There will be days when resentment and anger will raise its ugly head, but you must not allow it to; **be angry but do not sin (Ephesians 4:26). Resist the devil and he will flee from you (James 4:7). Sometimes we are tempted to retaliate and take revenge out on someone who has caused us hurt and grief, never allow yourself to entertain evil that may cause harm to yourself or someone else.** Begin a rebuilding process of trust; give yourself ample time to heal. Through love, faith, trust and obedience to Gods word, your marriage may be healed. **Never forget the words "I Love You." To God Be The Glory!**

Names and Lifestyles

What's in a Name? God changed "Abram" to "Abraham" and "Sarai" to "Sarah" (**Genesis 17:15**). Later Abraham became the father of many nations and they were blessed through him. **Names and lifestyles are important (Proverbs 22:1), especially when seeking a marriage partner**. It is important to know about the name and "Lifestyle" of the family you are getting into for a lifelong connection. You will not be alone in that connection. Her family will also play a key role in your marital relationship.

> ***You will not be alone in that connection. Her family will also play a key role in your marital relationship.***

Some people may disagree with me on this matter, however, with crime on the increase and felony convictions, **your whole lifestyle can change depending upon whom you are attached too.** A man or woman with a past felony or murder conviction will have many of their rights restricted. Breaking probation can land them right back in prison, and if children are involved, the spouse is left to support them alone. Consider the cost of the relationship and if you have the patience and resources to provide the support that you need. **Some individuals have been able to blend back into society and live successful lives**

through much support of the Church and their families. Consider the nature of the offense. Was violence involved? Have you observed a true change in the person who committed the offense? If the man you have formed a relationship with has a family history of preying on women, abuse and a violent behavior, you may want to weigh your options. If the woman you are considering as a potential spouse have had a history of drug abuse and several children by different men at an early age with what appears to be a family tradition, you may want to weigh your options. If the man you are considering for marriage have no formal or academic education and rarely have a job, you may want to weigh your options. **People do change however, generational curses can only change by the power of the Living God, Jesus Christ. Through God all things are possible. To God Be the Glory!**

Communicate!

Talk is cheap, but it's worth a fortune in a marriage. Good communication is a must! Show me a marriage without communication and I will show you a divorce in the making. We must communicate with God daily, letting him know the desires of our heart, he already knows, but he wants us to tell him or acknowledge who he is, that's the same example in marriage, we need to express our needs, desires and love for one another and do it often, **from the boardroom to the bedroom, talk to each other. What does good communication accomplish in a marriage? It builds trust, unity, understanding, desire and love. When you can talk to each other, barriers come down; you become an open book to your spouse. You should be able to talk about anything to the one you love.**

> ***When you can talk to each other, barriers come down; you are an open book to your spouse. You should be able to talk about anything to the one you love.***

There will be disagreements; good communication can help you get answers to difficult questions or situations. **Be patient; allow your relationship to grow through faith and experiences.** Have you ever noticed that two people who have gone through a traumatic experience together come out with a greater respect, love and admiration for one another, it is because they had to come together and ignore each other's differences in order to survive it, it became a spiritual connection. **That connection can be verbal or nonverbal and have no boundaries or distance between you. A husband or wife can be one hundred miles from each other and sense the spiritual welfare of the other.** In marriage you are one, **acknowledge one another and respect each other's opinion**. In making decisions, there may not be a right or wrong answer, **but there is a best answer**, go with the best answer after prayer and guidance by the Holy Spirit. **It does not matter who gives the best answer, you are in this marriage together. Men should appreciate a wife who possesses knowledge, wisdom and understanding. Women should appreciate a husband who respects her and regard her as his equal in the relationship, acknowledging her gifts, and using them often to build a loving, trusting and lasting relationship. Do not forget to say, "I love you." To God Be The Glory!**

When Love Began To Fade

Love between a husband and wife should be forever. At times we allow other things to interfere or become more important to us than our spouse **(Genesis 2:24) "Complacency, jealousy, selfishness, abuse, infidelity and money are key destroyers of marriages," we take for granted those things that are important in keeping our marriage active and vibrant. At times, it's good to be adventuresome and spontaneous in bringing about excitement in your relationship. Go out to dinner, take a trip or go see a good movie. The main thing is being involved in each other's lives on a daily basis. You should develop a mutual understanding when you need some time alone. The Bible speaks of it. While you are alone do not get drawn away into sin. Keep in touch; express your love for one another.** If you consider your spouse to be less important than yourself, you subconsciously exclude him from important aspects of your life.

> ***If you consider your spouse to be less important than yourself, you subconsciously exclude him from important aspects of your life***

If you value other relationships above that of your spouse, then you must redefine the purpose of your marriage and take inventory of yourself. Some people choose a career, or a job promotion that boosts their financial status, and as a result their relationship suffers and eventually dissolves. Relationships with children and other family members are sometimes chosen above that of their spouse, placing the spouse as the least important person or thing in their lives. **Of course this type of relationship will not stand. Your spouse deserves better.** You are denying him or her happiness with the one they have chosen to love until death do them part. That person is you! How selfish! Your husband deserves more. He wants you, he needs you and he loves you. You, on the other hand don't want him, need him or love him as he loves you. What a dilemma! It is a painful and destructive situation. **There is no easy way to deal with this type of relationship. Being self-serving has proven to be morally destructive.** At some point you must make a decision, either try to make it work or end it. **If that deep abiding commitment is not there from the beginning, then you should postpone your marriage and redefine your goals.** Before you do, consider the loss consider the gain. **To God Be The Glory!**

Why Do Marriages Fail?

Marriages fail because marriage is sometimes looked at, as a means of convenience to satisfy monetary and sexual needs. Some people marry because they do not want to be alone. **But, the real reason why marriages fail Is because most couples did not seek ye first the "Kingdom Of Heaven." When we seek God first, he said that he would add all things unto us.** Seek him first, then he will choose for you a spouse, and put you together as one for the Kingdom, thereby love is manifested, and **"Love is the fulfillment of the Law Of God"(Romans 13:10). The problem with the marriage covenant today, is that God is not included in their relationship. Divorce would practically be non-existent if we follow the "laws of God" in our marriages. Marriage between a man and a woman is honorable and binding and must not to be taken lightly. It was created for a lifelong commitment and laced with special privileges.**

> ***Divorce would practically be non-existent if we follow the Laws Of God in our marriages. Marriage between a man and a woman is an honorable institution and not to be taken lightly. It was created for a lifelong commitment and laced with special privileges.***

No one can be everything to one person. A husband may be your Knight in shining armor, however, through that armor is a mere mortal man incapable of perfection in the flesh. The woman becomes disappointed when she realizes that she did not marry the man of her dreams, likewise the man discovers the same truths. **What makes the marriage succeed is the realization that both partners have faults, compromise and sacrifice is necessary.** In the Old Testament, Moses gave a certificate of divorce because of the Hardness of man's heart. **A marriage must consist of a lot of forgiveness and compassion toward each other. *The Lord Says* the day that you hear my voice harden not your heart. Many marriages fail because someone Refuses to forgive, forget and submit.** Marriage according to scripture has a purpose in Gods creation. Many women, including Christian women are finding it difficult to meet and marry what they perceive as a good marriage partner. They are chaste, clean living and a model Christian. **But men are refusing that which is good, instead, they want that contentious woman (Proverbs 21:19) who resent their leadership; she won't work, won't cook, won't clean the home, disrespect him and calls it love and the husband accepts it. Lust is often confused with love. The difference between the two is that lust is fleeting and has no intrinsic value except the satisfaction of the flesh or self-gratification. Love is a life long commitment of the heart, soul and spirit. Love surpasses all things including our differences. Love brings together that which is common and uncommon, that which is familiar and unfamiliar, that which is liked and disliked. Love is the fulfillment of the Law Of God (Romans 13:10).**

Love is a lifelong commitment of the heart, soul and spirit. Love surpasses all things including our differences. Love brings together that which is common and uncommon, that which is familiar and unfamiliar, that which is liked and disliked. Love is the fulfillment of the "Law Of God" (Romans 13:10).

That is why it is so important to ensure that your relationship is based upon love and not lust! How do you know when it is love and not lust? **Remove the physical or material element that you favor most from the relationship and then ask yourself can your relationship survive without it.** That physical element can be sex, money, status or even physical appearance. If your answer is an honest yes, your relationship should survive. There are other factors that must also be considered, **such as emotional fulfillment.** Couples who have been married for many years often brag about their extensive union, most are honorable, however, some are dysfunctional with no real purpose except the sharing of a miserable life with one another. Their marriages are shrouded with lies, infidelities, hypocrisies, arguments and deception. Do you think God is pleased with that union? **If your marriage cannot be a positive role model for someone else's, keep it to yourself.** David tried to deal with Bathsheba without knowledge, Abraham tried to deal with Sarah without knowledge, Sampson tried to deal with Delilah without knowledge, they ALL failed! Adam tried to deal with Eve without knowledge, he failed. If these men had dealt with their wives according To the "Word of God" they would not have failed. **Knowledge of the word of God is the absolute truth and will prevail.** The bible says study and show thyself approved (2 Timothy 2:15). **There is no law against the true Word Of God. When you deal with a person because of love, you consider that person. You put them before yourself.** The Word of God tells us that we must love our wives as we love ourselves. No man, hated his own flesh (Ephesians 5:29). **Never take each other's love for granted; it's the little things that count the most.** Giving a back and foot massage to your wife after a hard days work, or calling your husband during the day to remind him not to forget to take his medicine, or the wife preparing his favorite meal the way that he likes it, not the way she wants it, but the way he wants it, that is love!!! And Love is the fulfillment of the "Law Of God". **Saying "I Love You" goes a long way. To God Be The Glory!**

The Submissive Wife (A Treasure To Her Husband)

The submissive wife is a woman of virtue whose presence in her home brings about love, peace, and harmony between herself her husband and children. She is forever alert to their needs and desires in the home and fulfills them with loving-kindness. She can be assertive, caring, and kind all at the same time. **She is rare and priceless! She is indeed a "Virtuous Woman"(Proverbs 31:10).** Her name is well noted in the community and her family is blessed. Her children and husband loves her and say that they are blessed. Her virtue has a profound effect upon her husband; she gladly submits to him and welcomes his leadership. **He loves her, honors her and listen to her when she speaks because on her lips is the law of kindness, gentleness, love and peace.** God placed a virtuous woman in my life and I love her dearly. **I didn't really know about the qualities of a virtuous woman until I read "Proverbs 31:10."** Tears began to flow down my face when I read it because I knew that I had never experienced a woman like her, until I met my wife Gloria. My eyes were open and I realized that other women in my life such as my mother and sisters were also virtuous women. **What is it like to be in love with a virtuous woman? Unlike anything a man will ever experience except a closer walk with God Almighty.**

What is it like to be in love with a virtuous woman? Unlike anything a man will ever experience except a closer walk with God Almighty.

However, he will never experience her true virtue until the two of them are in Christ Jesus and become true believers. Her virtue comes from God and is of "Spirit." As her husband he can only experience that virtue when he becomes a born again Christian. **God places a special anointing upon the Christian marriage and the husband will see the true "Holy and feminine spirit" of his wife in Christ Jesus.** Believe me, I see it in my wife because God is the head of our lives and our marriage. **Her touches will be different, her kisses, the way she feel, look and smell to her husband will be of a Spiritual connection**. ***She will be the most beautiful woman in the world to him and no other woman will compare because her beauty goes far beyond the physical appearance, her beauty comes from within and emanates outward.*** Everything she wears, the things she do too him for him and with him will be special in his eyes. **She is truly a Woman Of God! To God Be The Glory**!

A Moment to Reflect

If I talk too much, Lord please shut me up!

If I am selfish, Lord please help me to remove self

If I anger to easily, Lord please help me to be humble

If I cease to love, remind me of the greatest love of all

If I don't give, remind me of the greatest giver of all

If I am unthankful, remind me to give you thanks

If I am vain, remind me that you resist the proud

And If I am on the roadway to hell Lord please give me a Roadmap to heaven. Amen

My Rib, My Woman, My Wife

The Lord placed Adam in a deep sleep and performed the first operation for mankind. That operation led to the beginning of a most beautiful, joyous, wonderful and thrilling relationship. The Lord looked down upon Adam and said "It's not good that man should be alone, I will make him a helpmeet for him." Helpmeet means a helper, not a hindrance, When God created man; he also created that specific woman for him. God chose Eve for Adam. **Man's quest is to find that rib that God made for him from the beginning of time, (a man that finds a wife finds a good thing and obtain favor of the Lord)(Proverbs 18:22), some men find her right away, some take years, some a lifetime and some never finds her.**

> ***Man's quest is to find that rib that God made for him from the beginning of time (A man that finds a wife finds a good thing and obtain favor of the Lord (Proverbs 18:22). Some men find her right away, some take years, some a lifetime and some never finds her.***

How does a man find his rib? By seeking God first. The Lord said that men began taking women of their own choosing (Genesis 6:2),

the woman that God chooses for you have the right temperament and personality that agrees with yours. Everything falls in place; you will love her from the first time you meet. There will be no hesitation about her because God chose her for you. You will walk in agreement and serve the same God. So, how does a man who does not serve God find his rib? Because God gives us a choice, and variety; sometimes we choose wisely, sometimes we choose wrong even when God show us our helpmeet. **An unwise choice usually comes from the lust of the flesh, lust of the eyes and pride of life. By chance, we may choose wisely, the Holy Spirit will help us to discern that which is good and favorable in the eyes of God. A word of caution, ensure that your relationship is of a "spiritual connection" and not one of the flesh. Adam an Eve's relationship was of the "flesh" that led to their fall. A true spiritual connection is lasting, life long and wonderful. Seek it, breathe it and live it! To God Be The Glory!**

Intimacy In Marriage

Marriage is honorable in all and the bed is undefiled (Hebrew 13:4) Glory to God! This is a great and wonderful blessing from God, he allows us to enjoy the flesh without sin. **However, this enjoyment is only through the sanctity of marriage between a man and woman. Intimacy is wonderful when God put two people together. What two he put together, let not man split asunder (Matthew 19:6).** Love is expressed the way God intended for it to be, it is love without sin. **Fornication, adultery, homosexuality, lesbianism and any other sexual union that is not between a man and woman married to each other are of sin. True love in a marriage brings about true intimacy in the relationship. True lovemaking is delicious when it is undefiled. Intimacy should never be a selfish act, but an act of giving and receiving. We give love and receive love in its purest and intense manner.**

> ***Intimacy should never be a selfish act, but an act of giving and receiving. We give love and receive love in its purest and intense manner.***

Sensations are multiplied, every touch, every word spoken sparks a deeper desire to want to please and be pleased, all without sin. Adam and Eve probably had that relationship before the fall; their relationship was pure and uninhibited, because when **God asked Adam where was he, Adam replied we hid ourselves because we were naked; the Lord asked him, "Who told you that you were naked"? (Genesis 3:10-11)** you see nakedness was not a sin until Adam and Eve introduced sin into the world by disobeying God. I can imagine every touch, every word spoken was a prelude to Godly intimacy. **When we love each other in marriage, no one else will be allowed the benefits of sexual intimacy in our relationship. They will not be allowed to defile what God have made Holy and Honorable, that is, the sanctity of marriage. Your desire is to please God and each other. The husband's body belongs to the wife, and the wife body belongs to her husband (1 Corinthians 7:4). Do not misuse or abuse one another. Every lustful thought and every act of adultery or fornication can weaken and deteriorate the marital relationship between the husband and wife. Adultery does not require physical contact, adultery can be committed in the heart, (Matthew 5:27-28) guard your heart!** The "**Lust of the Flesh**" will raise its ugly head up once and awhile, however, love for God and your spouse will immediately extinguish the flames of sin and bring you back into a loving and spiritual relationship, under the watchful eyes of God almighty; which will keep you and sustain you. **Always remember to say, "I Love you," To God Be The Glory!**

Bringing Prosperity To Your Home

The Lord says be fruitful and multiply in our marriages, as a matter of fact he commands it! To be fruitful and multiply simply means be prosperous in all you do. **That means spiritually, physically, intimately and emotionally.** Using your God-given gifts to help edify the Church and glorify God in all that we do is serving him spiritually. Physically is presenting our bodies as a living sacrifice by remaining chaste and not abusing the body by committing fornication, adultery, using drugs and drunkenness. Intimately is remaining holy in loving and being loved. Emotionally is grounded in true worship, giving and receiving. Giving your time to the ministry, being a good spiritual leader who provides assistance and guidance to those in need and being a good husband or wife and a great father and mother to your children. Being prosperous in whatever we do. Being good stewards of our finances, and taking care of our families. **We must practice the law of giving and receiving (everyone that ask give). The Lord loves a cheerful giver. So how do we bring a continuous flow of prosperity to our homes? By always being conscious of "reciprocity," the act of giving and receiving. As a man soweth so shall he reap (Galatians 6:7).**

So how do we bring a continuous flow of prosperity to our homes? By always being conscious of "reciprocity," the act of giving and receiving. As a man soweth so shall he reap (Galatians 6:7)

Prosperity is no secret in the kingdom of God or among men. God made it plain and simple for anyone to follow. **Try me! He says and see don't I open the windows of heaven and pour you out a blessing you won't have enough room to receive it (Malachi 3:10).** What is the process of receiving these blessings? **We received them through obedience, tithes and offerings**. Can a man rob God? The Lord asked for only 10% of your earnings and a little assistance to the poor (offerings) who will always be with us. **Paying tithes is a blessing from God. Yes, it is a blessing because he has given us an avenue to get from him more than we deserve.**

Paying tithes is a blessing from God. Yes, it is a blessing because he has given us an avenue to get from Him more than we deserve.

He has given us a continuous flow of prosperity for pennies on the dollar. Where else can you find such great return on an investment? **Regardless of whether you are a Christian or not the Lord says give and he will give back to you. He rains on the just as well as the unjust. We all have access to God's fountain of wealth through tithes and offerings.** Your return will not always be monetary. It may be a reduction in costs, lowering your rent, car payment, or a lower insurance premium, a free vacation, and many spiritual blessings. The list can go on and on. Gloria and I pay tithes every pay period and reap the rewards. One dollar seems to spend like it's five. Our pockets are never empty. Don't get me wrong, there may be days when you come up short but God will make a way for you. Keep a continuous flow of prosperity in your home by giving to God first. **To God Be The Glory**!

Sustaining Your Marriage

With so many divorces and negative comments about marriage today, ***people still marry and the majority do so because they love each other, or at least they think they do*****! Once we are married we must begin a building process,** and **what we bring to the marriage depends on how well we can build it. It is important to establish trust and understanding from the very beginning. Trust is an absolute must in any marriage**. Once the level of trust has been established, we must begin to secure it. **How do we secure mutual trust? By being an open book to one another. Start by being honest and resolving issues before you get married; in other words "have no skeletons in your closet."** Never do things in your marriage that will arouse suspicion. **Suspicious behavior shuts down or intensifies the communication process in a negative way and places a strain on your marriage.** Demonstrate loyalty to your spouse by keeping private those things that she has expressed to you in secret. It is embarrassing to your spouse to find out the things she told you in private are now public information. **Never physically harm or verbally abuse your spouse. Do not compare past relationships with your present one regardless of whether they were good or bad.**

Never physically harm or verbally abuse your spouse. Do not compare past relationships with your present one regardless of whether they were good or bad.

You must discuss with your spouse, those things, that you consider are important in building and maintaining trust in your marriage.

Marriage is all about giving and receiving. It is a gift from God. He wants us to give love, show love and be love to each other. Always deal with your spouse in the "**Spirit of the Matter.** " **The Bible says there's no good thing in the flesh (Romans 7:18), and the Lord says not by might, but by my Spirit (Zechariah 4:6). Every successful marriage has a "spiritual connection" within that marriage.** Have you ever called each other at the same time, or think of the same thing at the same time? This is a spiritual connection; it says that you are on one accord and compatible with each other. **Things that are of the flesh are adultery, fornication, uncleanness, lasciviousness, idolatry, witchcraft, hatred, variance, emulations, wrath, strife, seditions, heresies, envying, murders, drunkenness and revellings (Galatians 5:19-21); never deal with your marriage pertaining to things of the flesh. Keep these things out of your marriage. However, the fruit of the Spirit is love, joy, peace, longsuffering, gentleness, goodness, faith, meekness and temperance (Galatians 5:22-23). Keep these in your marriage, for they will help to sustain it.** Remember in the Chapter "**Romancing The Love**", where I used the example of a river that if it flows in only one direction it eventually dries up. **Marriage must have a flow and love connection in order to thrive and survive, that flow and connection comes from God through you to your spouse. Godly love never fails. Love must flow in both directions, giving and receiving**. When love flows in both directions, it is **"Easy Love."** When God put two people together, there is no hesitation or doubt about their relationship and its purpose. **"Easy Love" is giving, caring, loving, receiving, forgiving, kind, compassionate, passionate, unselfish and thoughtful**. Include these things in your daily diet for a healthy marriage. And remember to say "I Love You," **To God Be The Glory!**

When Adversity Strikes Your Home

We all think that we should be able to live a happy and prosperous life. And sometimes we are not prepared when bad things happen to us. **We think that we are in control even when things seem out of control and your life is at a stand still.** At that time we must make a decision. We ask ourselves, what must we do and how are we going to handle the situation before us. **Regenerate your thinking! The Lord says be ye transformed by the renewing of your mind (Romans 12:2).** We must renew our thinking daily, and that thinking must be laced with faith and words of victory! Have you seen two fighters who are equally matched in strength and skill? One has the Spirit of Victory; he says I can defeat my opponent. The other has the spirit of fear. He says he may lose the fight because his opponent has never lost. Who do you think will win the fight! The one who is confident because he has no fear! **Fear weakens the power of the spirit.** Fear has cost many to lose who should have won. **For God have not given us the spirit of fear, but of power, and of love, and of a sound mind (2Timothy 1:7).** You do not have to be in the situation you are in; you can make it better, by the renewing of your mind. **Remember God is a God of plenty. Remember His promises. He says He will never leave you nor forsake you, remember His grace and mercy. Go into prayer and fasting and awaken the fight in you. God equipped you to fight and He says to put on the "whole armor of God." The whole armor is His Word, His promises and His Holy Spirit.** Think of the things that are good, acknowledge that they are good and use them. If you are suffering financially and behind in your bills, call those that you owe and tell them your financial status and that you will be late. Pay them as soon as possible. Be positive about finding a better job and pray first. Remember there are no situations so hopeless or so far gone that God cannot renew them. Trust in him, have patience that he will see you through. **Do not get angry or develop an attitude with your spouse because of debt, frustration, or anything else. The two of you must conquer this problem together. Keep your love and happiness alive no matter what comes against you or challenges you face.** If you have become disabled or have an illness in the family that's got you down or out of work; remember, **"That too shall pass."** Be strong for those of your family who are weak, for the bible says that **the strong ought to bear the infirmities of the weak (Romans 15:1).**

If you have become disabled or have an illness in the family that's got you down or out of work; remember, "That too shall Pass". Be strong for those of your family who are weak, for the bible says that the strong ought to bear the infirmities of the weak (Romans 15:1)

No one should try to go it alone. If the sickness is fatal, give the person comfort, go into prayer with them. Remove the sad faces; always look forward to a better day and improved circumstances. If this sound like a pep talk then maybe it is! Satan wants you in the wrong spirit and that is the "**spirit of defeat**!" God wants you in the right Spirit and that's the "**Spirit of Victory**!" Know that whatever the circumstances are, you have the Victory! And that is in Christ Jesus! **Give God Thanks, Give God The Glory, Now declare your victory today!**

-Greater is He that is in me, than he that is in the world (1 John 4:4)

-I will never leave thee nor forsake thee (Hebrew 13:5)

-The battle is not yours, but God's (2 Chronicles 20:15)

-Ask and it shall be given you, seek, and ye shall find (Matthew 7:7)

-The steps of a good man are ordered by the Lord (Psalm 37:23)

-Yea though I walk through the valley of the shadow of death I will fear no evil for thou art with me (Psalm 23:4)

-Son of man can these bones live? (Ezekiel 37:3)

God does not have wimps in his Army, but soldiers brave in battle: see (Zechariah 10:5)

***-Now awaken the Kingdom in you!* To God Be The Glory!**

Account-ability

Adam gave the Lord an excuse for his disobedience while in the Garden of Eden. His excuse was pointed toward Eve as causing him to do that which God had commanded him not to do. **We are quick to point fingers at the ones we love when in fact we are solely responsible for our failures and shortcomings.**

> ***We are quick to point fingers at the ones we love when in fact we are solely responsible for our failures and shortcomings.***

We are accountable for our actions in our marriages and relationships with others. The so-called **"Pass the Buck"** is common in our everyday lives. We blame traffic for being late for work. We blame the teachers for our children's poor grades; we blame the cigarette industry when we get cancer from smoking. We blame our spouses when we get caught in an unfaithful relationship; we are accustomed to blaming everyone except ourselves. **In our relationships we must stop making excuses for our own faults. Accept the truth, correct the problem and move on. Do not allow problems to simmer or remain a thorn in your relationship, because the problem will eventually lead to resentment and destruction. If not brought to an area of attention, problems**

will become a "silent killer." Bringing them to an area of discussion opens up a forum to correct or neutralize them. A sore, if remained untreated may become infected; if dealt with immediately, the healing process will begin. Expose the problem, expose the sin. The Lord tells us that He will remember our sins no more; then we must do the same for one another. **Do not be hypocritical about forgiveness and continue to harbor anger and resentment in your heart toward your spouse; that anger and resentment leads to abuse in a most provocative way (Ephesians 4:26).** Your spouse deserves better. We must look past each other's faults and see our needs, a need to be loved, cherished, honored, cared for and respected. **To God Be The Glory!**

Lie-ability

When Ananias and Sapphira lied to the Apostle Peter about the profits they acquired from the sale of their property they had no idea that the lie would lead to death and destruction **(Acts 5:5).** We must seek out our own salvation. **Ananias and Sapphira were one in marriage; you must also be one in righteousness.** God is a just God and no respecter of persons. **Your commitment to Christ should be above commitment to all others; be obedient to God no matter what the situation may be. Ananias was asked first, he lied and was killed.** Sapphira was given an opportunity to save her life by telling the truth; however, she chose to lie just like her husband. She was under no obligation to lie and her lie was voluntary. **"A wife who believes in righteousness, through her chaste conversation, and God given wisdom can be a sustaining pillar of life to her marriage."** Ananias and Sapphira could have prevented their death by simply "telling the truth." **Lying in a relationship can bring about extreme pain and anger when uncovered, and believe me; it will be uncovered at a most inopportune time.**

Lying in a relationship can bring about extreme pain and anger when uncovered, and believe me; it will be uncovered at a most inopportune time.

God said that liars will not enter into His kingdom and will have their part in the lake of fire **(Rev 21:8).** What causes a person to lie in a relationship? **Lying is perceived as a way to remain in control of a person, situation or thing. Lying is a form of control, whether it is for oneself or directed toward the other person**. When we lie in a relationship, we hide the truth about ourselves and our circumstances, which we perceive as a means of control. A husband who lies to his wife about an adulterous relationship may place his wife in harm's way. An adulterous wife may do the same to her husband. The wife or husband may become an unwilling victim of violence or deadly disease from a jealous lover of the spouse. Never place the one you love in such a predicament. **One lie leads to another and eventually loses its strength and influence. Once that is lost, the lie becomes a "shame" and the person loses all credibility**. Liars, however, can go on and on for years without conscience, consideration, or concern about the damage that they may cause. **For this reason, never, put your faith and confidence in the "natural man" (trust the spirit of the man).** How do you deal with a liar? In the "**truth,**" ask for proof of every lie told at the moment it is told, or suggest or recommend a course of action that works toward your advantage. Do not assume that "once a liar, always a liar," pray for that person. **True change comes through faith and prayer**. The Bible says that "The Truth Shall Make You Free." The truth helps you to regain control of your life, not to destroy it**. To God Be The Glory!**

It's All About "Attitude"

Attitudes can make or break a relationship; **a good attitude brings about a good relationship and possesses a positive outlook on life.** What is your attitude toward your relationship? Are you negative? Do you believe in your relationship? The Lord tells us to check ourselves to see if we are in the faith. **Our faith determines our attitudes.** We must also have faith that the Lord will direct our paths and change our attitudes toward one another. Do you show love without expectation of reward? Do you give without restrictions? Do you tell your spouse that you love her often? Do you constantly complain about her cooking? Moses gave a certificate of divorce because of the hardness of man's heart. **A hard cold heart can cause you to lose many blessings. The Lord says, "husbands be kind to your wives so that your prayers will not be hindered," (1 Peter 3:7).** Many marriages are suffering because of "**attitudes." The Lord will not bless pride, arrogance, or selfishness in a marriage.**

> ***Many marriages are suffering because of "attitudes." The Lord will not bless Pride, arrogance or selfishness in a marriage.***

The Lord turned Pharaoh's heart cold and made him pursue the children of Israel so that God could show them that He was their God, that He loves them and he would deliver them from their enemies. The hardness of Pharaoh's heart destroyed him and in your marriage, the hardness of your heart will do the same. **A hard cold heart or stubborn mind can turn God's blessings away from your marriage. Wickedness is a voluntary act. Arrest it and destroy it.** Do not let the sun go down on your wrath (Ephesians 4:26). Be angry but do not sin. **To God Be The Glory!**

Romancing The Love

Love is a universal language; it fuels the substance of life: **"For God so loved the world that He gave his only "Begotten Son" that whosoever believeth in Him shall not perish but have everlasting life" (John 3:16).** God is love, so love should be manifested everyday in our lives, give love, show love and be love. **Love is based upon giving and receiving. In order for love to be complete, it must flow in both directions. If it only flows in one direction, the source that it flows from dries up. A river flows and comes back to its beginning point, recycling and cleansing itself of debris as it flows. Once steady flow is established, the water comes clear and is good. Love must flow like rivers of running water, cleansing and replenishing the mind, body, spirit, and soul daily.** Desire your spouse, honor her, reverence him and keep the fires of passion burning between you. You say, "OK; but how?" Consider him first, think of ways to make him happy. Love him with your deepest passion; make him the King of his Castle. Speak the language of love to him at all times. What is the language of love? **"Honey, I love you; I miss you, I can't wait for you to get home. You are a smart man, a brilliant man." Buy him a favorite suit, socks, shoes; prepare his favorite meal, etc.** These are things that make your man feel like he is being loved. ***What is the secret of making and keeping him happy? PRAISE!! Praise him through good and bad times, and watch him develop into the husband that you will always admire and desire.***

What is the secret of making and keeping him happy? PRAISE!! Praise him through good and bad times, and watch him develop into the husband that you will always admire and desire.

Men love *PRAISE,* especially from the woman that loves him! Men, give your wife your undivided attention when she is with you and talking to you. She thirsts for love when you ignore her. *Tell her how beautiful and wonderfully made she is. She is like a flower that needs nourishment daily, that nourishment is your love! Do not neglect your flower, she is precious! The wife is fruit to her husband. She provides a nourishment of love, strength, peace and joy to his life. She is the fruit of his vine (his glory) and God is their source.* Tell her you love her often; use body language to express an outward signal of what is to come. ***The eyes are the mirrors of the soul, look into each other's soul and find the things you need, want and desire.* If you don't see them, then ask for them and expect to receive them. *It is your spouse's duty to give you what you need, deserve and desire* (1 Corinthians 7:3) (Ephesians 5:33).** Embrace and kiss each other tenderly, when appropriate. Do not entertain the spirit of jealousy, envy or selfishness in your relationship and in your walk with Christ. **Avoid negative people who disrespect, and dishonor marriage. Their spirits will attempt to invade and destroy yours. *You must protect your marriage at all times from negative and destructive influences.*** Do things together that both of you enjoy doing. Take frequent rides to favorite places or sites. This helps strengthen the bonds of your marriage. You began to learn and appreciate each other and each other's differences and it also adds to conversation, giving you memories to share and experience over and over again. **Complacency can destroy a marriage. Be active and vibrant in the things you do! Keep God in your life, and pray together often. Never, ever forget to say, "Honey, I Love You so Much!" To God Be The Glory!**

No "TV" In The Bedroom

Your bedroom should be a place of rest, relaxation and excitement void of distractions. The only objects of your affection in your bedroom should be each other. **Make it a habit of walking through your bedroom door leaving any and all distractions outside**. Small talk about your job, children, bills, shopping, car problems, noisy or nosey neighbors; the list goes on and on. Save it for another moment and time. And of course the television set! **Do not place a "TV" set in your bedroom, because it destroys valuable time, which the two of you need to harvest precious, intimate moments, with each other.** Our love life suffers because of our busy schedules. **Both partners usually have jobs that require long work hours and some involve working weekends.** Children must be cared for around the clock. And as a result, your intimate moments become hurried moments coupled with frustrations and worry. This in itself places a tremendous strain on your marriage and the intimate moments you need to keep it joyful and sustainable. **Your bedroom is for bonding and rebonding, charging and recharging establishing a sense of oneness with each other;** being fruitful and multiplying, desiring and being desired, needing and being needed, exclusive and being exclusively; get the point!!

Your bedroom is for bonding and rebonding, charging and recharging establishing a sense of oneness with each other; being fruitful and multiplying, desiring and being desired, needed and being needed, exclusive and exclusively, get the point!!!

Make your bedroom a "***den of love for loving***" where joy, peace, love and happiness are kindled. Love one another with your deepest passion: **this is not a time for inhibitions. If you feel your body is not the most beautiful, so what! It is the most beautiful to your spouse who loves you dearly. Let go and enjoy each other. To God Be The Glory!**

Defining Your Love

We define our love by its depth, brevity and clarity. How deep is your commitment to each other? Do you place other family members and friends before your husband or wife? **You are a team and you must function as one. A house divided will not stand (Mark 3:24-25).** Do not allow other family members to drive a wedge between your relationship with your spouse. Let them see and understand your commitment toward one another, and that you are on "***one accord,***" this also includes your children. How serious do you take your vows and do you honor them? The Lord commands us to keep our vows made to him and it is important to keep them with each other. A vow is a binding promise and agreement and must be taken seriously. **A true marriage should be a permanent covenant and rest upon a foundation of Love, faith, trust, honor, compassion, compromise, sacrifice and obedience to the Lord.**

> ***A true marriage should be a permanent covenant and rest upon a foundation of love, faith, trust, honor, compassion, compromise, sacrifice and obedience to the Lord.***

Are you in your relationship for the long haul, are, are you subject to abandon it at the first sign of trouble? How far does your love extend? If your husband wants to relocate to a different state or country, are you willing to follow him wherever he goes, even if it means giving up some of your comfort or change of lifestyle? **Fear of the unknown can hinder many blessings**. Can you clearly identify the depth of your understanding of each other? **Express your desires and work out a plan to bring them to pass. Are your goals clearly defined**? Are you going to buy a new house in five years, Increase your financial status or buy a new car? And are you in agreement with one another and have clearly defined your goals? Do you possess and value the same Christian beliefs? Have roles been established in your relationship? Does children play a part now or in the future? Marriage is a wonderful experience, however, because it is a lifelong commitment, it is advisable to seek marital Christian counseling first**. To God Be The Glory**!

Kinfolks and Conflicts

Family members can be a blessing or a curse to your relationship; ensure they bring blessings instead of curses. One thing in particular, is that family members in conflict with you or your spouse can cause devastating consequences. Children will be separated from the relatives they love and support from family members will be non-existent. **So, what do you do when this happens? Nothing! Absolutely nothing, leave it alone. Don't try to fix anything right away. Love your spouse. Give him the support he needs. Stand by him, and let him know that you love him, and nothing will separate you, but God,** (Let not man split asunder), give it time; conflicts have a way of burning themselves out if you don't fuel the fire. Be friendly, courteous and avoid arguments. **Avoid family members who are argumentative, heavy drinkers, drug users, combative, envious, and jealous.** Do all you can to keep the peace, remember to them you are the problem; make yourself an invisible problem. Pray about your circumstances, do not recompense evil for evil. **Do not engage in the "Finger Pointing" Syndrome**. The tongue is hard to tame. **There is death and life in the power of the tongue (Proverbs 18:21).** So, who comes first. You made a vow to your spouse and should possess a special love for him. **If you are not willing to forsake all others, then you should postpone marriage until you are willing to do so.** A great majority of spouses place their relatives above the place of their spouse, which is a grave mistake. **Marriage is a very intimate arrangement and your marriage partner share things with you that your relatives should not.**

Marriage is a very intimate arrangement and your marriage partner share things with you that your relatives should not.

Your spouse can hurt you the most or make you the happiest above all relatives. When Gloria and I married, it was understood by all, that we came first before anyone else but God! and yes, that includes children. Your relatives; however, do play an important part in your lives, of course you still love them, you still honor them, **but your spouse and family comes first! (1 Timothy 5:8). It is a very hard balancing act, but with God it is very easy.** Consider the lions and how the lionesses hunt for food instead of the big male lion; reasoning is because he was much slower and tired quickly. When the lionesses would bring down prey, they would allow the big male to eat first, this ensured that he would remain strong to father and protect the "Pride"(family of lions). If the animal kingdom can have a family structure, then so can man. Remember, God created the man first, without him there would be no women or children. The husband and wife is always first, this is where blessings come into the marriage, believe me, no one will go lacking, **your children will be taken care of by both parents and well nourished because your house is in order. Infants and toddlers are your top priority and require many personal sacrifices.** Sometimes they may either destroy or build a stronger relationship depending upon certain circumstances and challenges. For this reason, **a strong bond between the husband and wife should be established before children are introduced into the marriage.** Loving parents would automatically provide for their children even if it meant personal sacrifices. Word of advice, **"Keep children out of adult affairs." Do not neglect your duties toward your spouse simply because your children selfishly demand your attention.** Do not allow children to decide whom you fall in love with or marry. They certainly wouldn't allow you to decide for them! **So, who comes first? God comes first, then your spouse, children, and all others. Keep it that way and your a marriage will last. To God Be The Glory!**

Ex's

Breaking up with someone you love can be a traumatic experience. For whatever reason, the breakup should be a learning experience and another chapter of your life stories; and should bring about closure of that relationship. Some people play a cat and mouse game with each other's heart by continuously breaking up and making up; **and on occasion, include an innocent party in their game, destroying their self esteem and even their lives.** The innocent party find themselves caught in a web of lies, hypocrisy and deceit; she want to believe the lies but her heart tells her to move on.

> ***The innocent party find themselves caught in a web of lies, hypocrisy and deceit. She wants to believe the lies but her heart tells her to move on.***

She hopelessly feels that she is the one woman who can change him and is drawn deeper and deeper into his web. She desire a change in her life and seek that change through prayer; and God answers, however, her EX suddenly reappears in her life; that old flame begin to burn again, so now she is unsure about her present relationship, she began to find fault in that person that God have sent her. She thinks she never had closure and just need to know if there is something still there. Sounds familiar? If the relationship resulted in divorce, or some other reason, it is not likely that coming back together will make anything different, especially if a "Born Again," experience was not made. **That vicious cycle of pain will start all over again!** Sometimes it's good to burn bridges behind you. "Lots wife" looked back and was turned into a pillar of salt because she could not detach herself from the sin that conquered her heart. My response to you is, **don't do it!! Don't look back.** The Lord says do not let man split asunder and beware "the wiles of the devil," he is crafty, he is there to steal, kill and destroy, and he will destroy what you have with your newly ordained relationship that the Lord have blessed. The devil see your blessings before you do, does a dog return to his vomit **(2 Peter 2:22) It didn't work then, what make you think it will work now.** Dismiss the thoughts and go on with your new relationship. **To God Be The Glory!**

Until Death Do Us Part

Marriage is a life long commitment. We must be ever careful when choosing our partners; man instituted "until death do us part"; God did not place such a burden upon mankind, he gave us an understanding of "**His Will**" and purpose for marriage, and does in-fact, allow us to divorce when the marriage covenant between a man and woman or God have been broken. **A wife that is used as a punching bag by her husband gives new meaning of "until death do us part," she must depart from her husband in order to live. A physical death is not the only death that a marriage can suffer; a spiritually dead marriage is just as painful as the physical.** If we are in Christ Jesus we are a new creation: old things have passed away in our lives, and we have become new **(2 Corinthians 5:17).** Christ is foremost, and everything and everyone else is next. If you are in a marriage that denies your worship of God, go into prayer and fasting, the Lord will move upon your situation, and resolve the conflict. He may free you from that marriage. Jesus says, if you are not willing to leave mother, father sister, brother, husband or wife for my namesake, you are none of my disciples **(Luke 14:26)**. **Do not let an evil person cause you to lose your salvation, married to them or not!** The Lord says, "I hate divorce," if you are truly in Christ, There should never be a need or reason for the divorce, it is a heart felt decision. the Lord says, my children perish for lack of knowledge. **Divorce should never be for a desire of the flesh, but a renewing of the Spirit.**

Divorce should never be for a desire of the flesh, but a renewing of the spirit.

The bible says there is no good thing in the flesh. **Man divorce because of the lust of the flesh, lust of the eyes and the pride of life. Until death do us part have its merits. It means after all of the love, sacrifices, trials and tribulations that I have had to endure, my love still burns with a fervent fire and I still love and admire that person that God have chosen for me as my marriage partner, and I will love that person until the day that I die. To God Be The Glory!**

Constructive Criticism

We begin relationships hoping that the love, joy, peace, excitement and companionship remain steadfast forever, and regardless of how wonderful, vibrant and beautiful our relationships may be, at some time in our lives there will be disagreements. How we handle those disagreements will determine the stability and survivability of our marriage. Here are some important factors to consider that may help you remain steadfast in your marriage. **First, give yourself time to realize and recognize the problem at hand. Do not immediately react to the situation unless warranted. Pray first asking the Lord for a calm, meek and understanding spirit**. The Lord will give you answers to difficult questions; He will prepare your heart. Then place your problem before you and your spouse. Address it, engage it and dissect it together. **Regardless of who is at fault, address the problem, not the person.**

> ***Regardless of who is at fault, address the problem, not the person.***

This in itself will save a lot of arguments and ill feelings toward one another, and you will find the problem less difficult to solve. For example: the dishes need to be washed and the kitchen cleaned.

However, both of you work! Address the problem, and then decide your solution. Sometimes we must be assertive when dealing with and finding solutions to some problems. Let the Holy Spirit lead you in your assertiveness. **Adultery, physical, emotional abuse and sexual crimes must be addressed to the person and dealt with in a face to face interaction, for we are not dealing with material objects but people.** Objects cannot express why they did it, they cannot say forgive me, or I don't want this marriage anymore. **It is absolutely imperative to have a solid foundation of love and trust in your marriage in order to survive some situations listed above.** If love and trust is not present in your marriage, addressing the problem will be very difficult. You will either heal, tear down, provoke, build-up or end your relationship, so tread carefully. Be empathetic. ***Seek Christian counseling involving situations that are beyond your ability, knowledge and understanding.*** **To God Be The Glory!**

True Love, It's A Done Deal

True love in your marriage is a spiritual experience that cannot be explained; but felt with an experience of joy, peace, understanding, compassion, empathy and oneness with one another. **There are marriages that have never experienced true love because they won't include God in its making and survivability.** Before seeking marriage, go into prayer asking God to prepare you for your mate and your mate for you. That preparation is the foundation for your marriage.

Before seeking marriage, go into prayer asking God to prepare you for your mate and your mate for you. That preparation is the foundation for your marriage.

You want to ensure its survivability through good and bad times. **God does not make mistakes. When he put two people together in holy matrimony, it's a "done deal," and no weapon formed against it shall prosper. When true love is present in a marriage, it is felt and experienced. Understanding is always present; oneness with one another is inseparable. All that you do is for the glorification of the "Kingdom Of God.**" And all that you experience in your marriage is about true love. My wife Gloria and I experience true love daily because we prayed first, asking God to prepare us for each other. God prepared us and gave us the desires of our hearts and much more than we asked for! **True love is eternal. True love can never be faked; even an animal knows when it is being loved. If you only feed it and never hold it or touch it and simply walk away, eventually it will die from loneliness. True love is not selfish but giving, it is not abusive but tender in loving and caring. It is faithful and true, bears no animosity but meekness and understanding. If you want true love in your marriage, seek God first! To God Be The Glory!**

Words To Live By

-There are no marriages in heaven, enjoy yours here on earth

-Give 110 percent, so when you are not at your best, you're still giving more than the rest

-Where there is love, there is also peace

-Where there is hope, there is also victory!

-An act of kindness turns away wrath

-Honor your wife; Reverence your husband

-Take a moment to say "I love you," for nothing can be uttered from the grave

-As you say it, so shall it be in your heart, control your tongue

-A family that Prays together, is inseparable

-Resist the devil and he will flee from you

-Beauty is the glowing of the heart, if there is no glow, there's no beauty

-Do not let the sun go down on your wrath

-A heart that is full of joy, peace and happiness, is also full of love!

-Whatever things are honorable whatever things are of virtue do these things

-A heart that is full of love is also full of forgiveness and will do you no harm

-Love is the fuel that ignites the flames of passion in your heart!

-The battle first starts in the mind, guard your mind

-Go to sleep every night with a clear conscience, so you

Won't wake up in a pile of mess

Love, Passion and Desire, The Ultimate Fuel For Your Marriage

Your marriage must possess the elements of Love, Passion, and desire in order for it to thrive. That love is a love for Christ, love for people, a love for each other and looking past our weaknesses. A love for Christ is loving him with all your mind, heart, soul and spirit. A love for people is respecting others and their opinion and speaking words of encouragement and helping each other in times of need. Love is a conqueror and cannot be defeated. **No matter what the problem or situation may be, if love is present it can be overcome. Love gives us strength during times of weakness and understanding in times of confusion.**

> ***No matter what the problem or situation may be, if love is present it can be overcome. Love gives us strength during times of weakness and understanding in times of confusion.***

I was in great distress after my father died and one day I asked the Lord to just let me feel his love upon me; at that moment a great feeling overcame me, it was so powerful that I thought I was going to die! I began to feel and understand what God's love was all about and that mortal man was not capable of feeling God's Love completely until he's changed from mortal to immortal. **God's love in its entirety is too powerful for mortal man to withstand. He would die instantly from its force!** Bring the sum total of your love into your marriage and see miraculous things happen! **Be passionate in all that you do and do it for the Lord. Your Passion should be a passion for life, a passion to please God, a passion to please your spouse. Passion drives life and life drives Passion; whatever you do be passionate about it!** The threads of life signifies a desire to live, **Jesus gave us a thread of life and that thread is love, hope, faith, worship and obedience through the Holy Spirit.** His desire was to please the Father. Our desire is to please him. We please him in worship, in the way we live, act and treat one another. **Treat your spouse with love, joy, compassion, peace and understanding. Always give an ear of understanding and a heart of compassion with love being the ultimate fuel. To God Be The Glory!**

The Cornerstone of Your Marriage

Marriage has a purpose in our lives and in society. People don't get married just to be married. People marry because of love, respect, admiration, closeness, togetherness and happiness. Sometimes we marry for the wrong reasons and our expectations are above that which is actually obtainable. We vow to that person we love to honor them, cherish them, and be with them through sickness and in health, rich or poor. And to most couples those words are true, but to others they are just a formality echoed at a wedding ceremony. What makes marriage a success or failure? **Traditions, Attitudes, and Beliefs**: Our traditions have a direct effect upon our marriages. If our traditions differ from that of our spouse, compromise may be necessary. If you are traditionally Baptist and your spouse is Catholic, differences toward worship may cause problems. Ensure that the person you intend to marry are reading from the same pages that you are. If a man believes that the woman's place is in the home and he is unemployed but she has a job offer, a conflict of interest may arise. Get to know that person whom you intend to marry before you go to the altar. **Marriage is a God thing**! So it stands to reason to seek him first before you seek your helpmeet. **Make Christ the cornerstone of your marriage**. **When you build a marriage upon Christ it will stand any test of time, trials or tribulations.**

Make Christ the cornerstone of your marriage. When you build a marriage upon Christ it will withstand any test of time, trials or tribulations.

Knowledge of the word of God and guidance by the Holy Spirit will give you a wonderful and blissful marriage. As children of the true and living God we can take all of our problems to him, he wants us too! Whether it's financial, spiritual or physical, take your problems to Christ. **The husband as the leader of the home have a great ally in Christ.** This makes the husband one of the most powerful men on earth because he is of the kingdom that is never ending. He is of a kingdom where all needs are met. **A family that worships God is a family that shines as a light in darkness.** Your heart is pure, caring, loving and submissive to the word of God. ***The lust of the flesh, lust of the eyes and the pride of life have no power in a God ordained marriage.*** You love when you feel you are not being loved, you forgive where there appears to be no forgiveness, **the wife of a God fearing man have nothing to fear!** Because God is the head of his life and he listens to God and receive guidance from him. **Blessed are the man and woman who consecrate their marriage in the name of the Lord.** Through Christ your marriage is sanctified (set aside) for his purpose, receive salvation (protection from sin) and justified (made righteous). Let Christ be the Cornerstone Of Your Marriage. **Marriage is a good thing! To God Be The Glory!**

When Divorce Is Your Only Option

Read This First!

Divorce is never a good thing, but sometimes a necessary thing. It's not a good thing because although it may set you free from harm, danger, violence or even death; someone had to suffer. The emotional scars can run deep, physical abuse bears the outside scars but bigger scars remain inside. If children are involved they are thrust into an emotional battle they are not equipped to deal with. Their lives will be changed and they may be forced to choose between two people they love dearly. **The Lord says "I hate divorce," because God is love and if love is manifested in your marriage, coupled with a deep commitment and desire for one another, it will not happen. For this reason it is very important to seek God in your life before and after marriage,** ***seeking him first give you a renewing of mind, soul and spirit and takes you away from the natural realm of man, which is his life "according to the flesh," but now you are in the Spirit.*** **The Bible says that the first man was of the flesh and the second of the Spirit and that second man is Jesus Christ. You must be born again. Your marriage is a "born again experience," you experience new things in your life, and this is what makes it unique and favorable in the eyes of God.** Marriage should be like good soil that brings forth good fruit such as obedient children, prosperity, kindness, and love toward your neighbors, giving freely to those in need. **We must realize that our lives are fragile and we are all capable of making mistakes and bad decisions. But through all the pain, through the storm of resentment, unfaithfulness, lies, abuse and deception; God commands us to love and forgive one another. Forgiveness comes from the "spirit" and not from the "flesh." The flesh cannot forgive! Only the Spirit can show an act of forgiveness. This is why it is so important to deal with the person who offended or betrayed you in the "Spirit of The Matter." The spirit is a heart felt experience, heart and spirit go together. God deals with mankind in "Spirit and in Truth." Always deal with your spouse in "Spirit and In Truth." Never do anything you feel a need to lie about. *Lying destroys the integrity of your relationship with your spouse*. Betrayal can cause many responses. Anger, revenge, resentment, depression, jealousy and other forms of destructive behavior are common. If you feel like crying, then cry. Sometimes the hurt may seem unbearable. The Lord says he will never allow anything to come upon us that we cannot bear. Go to him and give your hurt and pain to the Lord Jesus Christ. He is sitting on the right hand of the "Father" making intercessions for us! He can help you bear the pain and take it away. The heart is the soul of a person, the Bible says that the eyes are the mirrors of the soul, if the eyes are spiritually dark, so is everything else. What changes the mind about divorce: prayers, faith, compassion, agreement, love, forgiveness and understanding.** If either element is missing divorce may happen. First of all forgive and seek guidance from the Lord through prayer; <u>read my prayers in the back of the book</u>. **Both must agree that you want to keep your marriage and make it work. Immediately cease with the blame. Advise relatives and friends that you and your spouse need some time alone. Exclude everyone else from your marriage except your pastor. Go into prayer and fasting.**

Immediately cease with the blame. Advise relatives and friends that you and your spouse need some time alone. Exclude everyone else from your marriage except your Pastor. Go into prayer and fasting .

Sometimes friends and relatives take sides, adding fuel to an already volatile situation. It's your problem, so try and deal with it. God is all you need as a Father, friend, judge, counselor, mediator, healer and Pastor. He can restore what you or others cannot! There is no crisis in a marriage that is so far gone that God cannot restore it! The question is, do you want your marriage to work? Do you still love each other? ***Then work on the love that you have left. Remember those things that made love happen between you and your spouse and began to rebuild on them. Read the "7 keys To A Successful Marriage" out loud to each other.*** Tear down bridges of anger, resentment, hate, revenge and selfishness through undying love and commitment toward one another. Also, a major problem is that one spouse may feel totally innocent of what's causing their marriage to fail. If you feel that way, fine, ask for forgiveness anyway; it takes two in a marriage to get to the stage of divorce. **Husbands must take the leadership role in the forgiveness process even if he feels that he is not at fault. He is the leader in the home and should lead by example. The so-called "breaking the ice" is what he needs to accomplish and initiate an open forum with his wife and or children if any is involved. His act of leadership displays love, compassion, empathy and strength to his family. He should go into prayer first for strength, knowledge, patience and wisdom about his family's problem.** Also, Consider Christian counseling. Christian counseling is a good thing; the counselor can serve as a mediator between the husband and wife especially if hostility toward one another is present. **The final stage is understanding, this includes the healing process. If you can understand why you got to the decision of divorce then you can begin to heal. Understanding is a seasoning of the heart, soul and spirit of the person, and those three become one; and when they become one, you and your spouse are in agreement, and the decision should be final and binding. Divorce or stay together.**

Understanding comes by communication. Do not allow anger, resentment, hate or outside influences to cause you to develop a cold heart and turn away from God and each other. You may need some time alone, spend it in prayer and fasting. **Fasting is wonderful for difficult decisions.** Whatever decision you make, realize that changes whether good or bad will take place in your life, adjustments take time, healing takes time. Remember to say the words "**I Love You,**" for by doing so; you can rekindle the flames of love, passion and desire in your marriage. **To God Be The Glory!**

Why Am I Lonely?

Loneliness is a state of mind that places your soul and spirit in bondage. The Lord says it is not good for man to be alone (man and woman). He said that he came to give us life and give it to us more abundantly. The Lord never intended for you to go it alone. So why are you alone? Because you chose to be! Loneliness is a self-inflicting action. Loneliness can also be contributed to a lack of understanding either from yourself or another person. You can be married and still be lonely. Marriage does not guarantee companionship. Two people must have something in common, you must be in agreement.

> ***You can be married and still be lonely. Marriage does not guarantee companionship. Two people must have something in common you must be in agreement.***

Loneliness comes in all shapes and sizes. Anyone can become lonely, including children. Children cannot express their need and desire for love the way adults can. Parents must ensure that their children receive a constant nourishment of love and care on a daily basis. If you are board in a relationship before marriage, more than likely you'll be bored in the marriage. **That is why you seek God first to ensure that you have the right person for the rest of your life.** Seek and develop understanding through communication; communicate, communicate, and communicate. What do you desire in your life? What do you intend to accomplish? God created you for a purpose, find and seek your purpose through Him. The Lord says to examine yourselves whether ye be in the faith (2 Corinthians 13:5). **If you isolate yourself, you cannot receive the love, companionship and joy that life brings through Christ Jesus. When a predator seeks its prey, he isolates it from the rest of its family; he then attacks the prey and eventually kills it if it does not find an avenue of escape. Satan isolated Eve from Adam and caused her to be the first in transgression (1 Timothy 2:14)**. The Lord says that we are like sheep for the slaughter, do not isolate yourself. Do not give yourself a "pity party." People get addicted to drugs, join gangs, cults and even commit suicide because of loneliness and a need to belong. Cast all of your problems upon the Lord. He will redeem you and set you free. The Lord will give you strength to raise you up and live. **How do you break the bondage of loneliness? through prayer. Pray for love, understanding, joy, companionship and peace in your life. Two are better than one. Marriage is a good thing in the Lord**. He says seek Him first, and **He will add** all other things unto you. He says he will even give you the desires of your heart according to "His Will" and purpose.. If you desire happiness, a husband, a wife or a friend, ask the Lord. Ask Him to remove the loneliness and bring joy and peace into your life. **To God Be the Glory!**

Special Note to Men

When the Lord brought Eve to Adam, Adam took on a great responsibility. He not only had to see to the earthly affairs that God had commanded him to do, but he had to take on a leadership role of great importance. Adam was a natural man, and the natural man does not understand the things of God; **Adam in his natural state, could not discern the consequences of his disobedience to God. Had he waited until God gave him the Spiritual (Holy Spirit), he would not have failed.** Adam failed as a leader and caused dire consequences to the entire human race. God has called men to be leaders in their homes and we are failing our families at an alarming rate. **The Lord says, "my people are destroyed for lack of knowledge" (Hosea 4:6). Men are commanded to acquire knowledge.** Our problem as men is that we do not acquire the necessary knowledge and skills to assume the leadership role in our homes. **We marry being unequipped to raise a family, we do not learn how to deal with our wives and chastise our children with loving-kindness. In order to be a husband, a father and a leader in our homes we must first prepare ourselves through education, mentoring and church**. that preparation began from the time that we were in diapers until marriage. **If we find ourselves unprepared there is still hope, that hope is in Christ Jesus and the Holy Spirit who will lead you, guide you and teach you.** Education gives us the ability to take care of our families. Mentoring gives us the necessary skills to deal with our wives and children. The Church gives us the spiritual guidance and support that we need to sustain our families, **and Christ is the overseer of it all! " Marriage is a Spiritual union." There is no good thing in the flesh; we must be able to connect with a power much greater than that of the "natural man." That power is Jesus Christ**. Christian men must remember that God made man in his own image after his own likeness, **we are to glorify God in all that we do**, that includes the way we deal with people in our everyday lives. **The Bible says whatsoever things are true; whatsoever things are honest, whatsoever things are just, think on these things (Philippians 4:8). Always deal with people in the "Spirit of the Matter," in other words look beyond the physical and deal with the inner being of the person.**

> ***Always deal with people in the "Spirit of the Matter," in other words look beyond the physical and deal with the inner being of the person.***

Believe me, you will experience different and deeper interactions with that person. Examine your faith and obedience to God daily. Communication is your most valuable asset. Regardless of your level of education, good oratory skills will get you into doors normally reserved for the elite. God communicates with us in all that we do. In the book of **Genesis,** Scripture says" **and God said, and it was good." Ensure that what you say is good. Your words will not return back to you void, and they will do what you send them to do. Education includes more than just academic knowledge. First acquire knowledge of yourself, know your limitations and build on them.** Learn survival skills, economic knowledge, financial knowledge, stocks and bonds; read your Bible and communicate with God daily. Men also learn from other men. **Find a good mentor in your church, your Pastor is a good start, he should possess years of experience in his calling and is outstanding in the community. Older men who are respected and revered in your community are also good role models to follow. Your spiritual health and well-being is extremely important, attend church services regularly. The way**

we communicate with our family determines successes or failures. That is why it is extremely important to develop good communication skills. A solid foundation of education, worship and belief in a higher power **(God)** will prepare you for the bride that God has prepared for you from the beginning of time. Sure you will have disagreements, but with God in the midst of your marriage you will succeed. **To God Be the Glory!**

Loving Your Wife

As men we must understand that love always comes from the heart and seeking love is a heart felt experience. **Loving your wife is also a heart felt experience. We must love them with all of our heart, soul and spirit. In order to do this, we must love God first above all things.** Loving God gives men strength; compassion, knowledge, wisdom and understanding that only God can give us. This allows men to be able to love those whom he has authority over and to love them with gentleness, compassion, wisdom, understanding and loving-kindness. Your wife is part of you. **There must be a connection that separates your relationship with your wife above anyone else. That's why Adam says that a man shall leave his father and mother and cleave to his wife and they shall be one flesh (Genesis 2:24). We share intimate moments with her to strengthen the bonds of love and marriage. How wonderful to embrace love with love, Godly love, that the two of you live and thrive in together! She should be the most beautiful, wonderful, loving and graceful woman you will ever experience, and you can make that happen by loving her, respecting her, honoring her, listening to her, understanding and taking care of her needs and desires according to your abilities.**

She should be the most beautiful, wonderful, loving and graceful woman you will ever experience and you can make that happen by loving her, respecting her, honoring her, listening to her, understanding and taking care of her needs and desires according to your abilities.

Always possess a forgiving heart, full of gentleness and loving kindness, never trying to control her, which leads to destruction in a relationship. Let God be the foundation for which your marriage rest upon. To God Be The Glory!

Loving Your Husband

When Eve looked upon Adam for the first time she realized that she was his Glory, for she was the only creation that God created that was compatible with him. When God created man he also created another need in man and that need was for a helpmeet, a woman. She was created to be a helper to her husband and to follow his lead. **She is the "Glory Of The Man,"(1 Corinthians 11:7) The Glory Of her husband.** She was to be part of the order of God's Universe. She was created to achieve, develop and manifest a God given Kingdom here on Earth with her husband. And she was to accomplish her purpose by being submissive to the "Word Of God." **Being submissive is an act of love and obedience to God. When a woman is submissive to her husband she opens channels of blessings. Their marriage receives honor and favor from the Lord.**

> ***Being submissive is an act of love and obedience to God. When a woman is submissive to her husband she opens channels of blessings. Their marriage receives honor and favor from the Lord.***

The Lord will not bless disorder in the home (1 Timothy 3:5). To submit to your husband says that you love him; you trust him and believe in what he is doing and what he represents. You are there to praise him when no one else does. Make him feel like he is loved and special in your life and to create an atmosphere of trust. **Many women find it difficult to submit to a man whom she perceives as unworthy or who have not earned her respect.** Many men are ill equipped to deal with a woman's intellect. In a relationship she thrives on emotions and he thrives on logic. What makes the relationship work is a balance between the two. They both possess equal amounts of emotions and logic. Sarah called her husband Abraham, lord, not that he was her lord; but out of love, respect and honor as the leader of their home. If you truly love him, submitting to him would be a pleasurable experience. **Loving your husband is feeling secure about yourself and secure about your relationship with him. The Bible tells the older women to teach the younger women how to love their husbands (Titus 2:4)**. In other words how to treat him and submit to his authority. The problem is that they themselves never learned or obeyed the "Word of God" about their role in marriage. **Submitting to your husband must be a spiritual connection. The Bible teaches us that the spirit indeed is willing but the flesh is weak (Matthew 26:41).** Love your husband, honor and respect his position in the home. Allow him the opportunity to lead and support his efforts. **To God Be The Glory!**

Marriage, Money and Education

The Bible says that money is the root of all evil, not money is evil. Money is simply an exchange of a valuable instrument for getting those things that help us live a more comfortable life and without it our lives can become uncomfortable. The Bible speaks of money in both blessings and curses. The Lord tells us to use it wisely, be good stewards of it and not to become greedy with its use. People have fought and died for money. It can make your life more comfortable but sometimes at a great cost. **Being wealthy can pose many problems; it causes people to lie about their feelings toward you. Is it love or is it money? A lot of money poses many problems; never allow it to become your God, never allow it to replace others in your life.** Money cannot love you back; it cannot ask you how are you feeling today? It cannot cuddle up with you on a cold winter night. It cannot kiss you or caress you and tell you how beautiful or how handsome you are.

> ***Money cannot love you back; it cannot ask you how are you feeling today? It cannot cuddle up with you on a cold winter night. It cannot kiss you or caress you and tell you how beautiful or how handsome you are.***

Everyone wants his or her needs and desires met; education is a vehicle for that to happen. ***However, there are no guarantees in our lives that an education will fulfill our desires. What fulfills our desires are a deep sense of commitment to our purpose and a desire to become all that we can be in reflecting our Creator.*** **Seek ye first the Kingdom of God and all his righteousness, and all these things shall be added on to you (Matthew 6:33). To God Be The Glory!**

Must I Go It Alone?

The term **"pulling your own weight"** is very important in a relationship. If one partner find themselves carrying the relationship while the other partner just go along for the ride it creates an air of resentment and confusion. The relationship suffers from lack of involvement and participation**.** You are there for each other, to build, tear down and lift up. If both partners need to be employed in order to take care of their needs, both must share that responsibility. Jesus said my Father and I are one. The Father was in heaven, Jesus on earth, everything Jesus did was for the kingdom. What if he had just sat back and did nothing for the kingdom? **A kingdom divided will not stand and neither will a home (Matthew 3:24-25).** You are responsible to help make your spouses life better. Do all you can do to bring joy, happiness, love and peace into their lives. **The Bible says a man who does not take care of his own family is worse than an infidel (1 Timothy 5:8).**

> ***The bible says a man who does not take care of his own family is worse than an infidel (1 Timothy 5:8).***

Take care that you do not abuse your substances of life (faith and abilities). The Lord divides to us gifts on an individual basis. We ought to use those gifts to help each other to glorify and edify the kingdom of God. Use your gift or gifts to help build a long-lasting and loving relationship in your home. If you cannot find employment, pray that the Lord will fulfill your needs and act on your circumstances. **Your enemy of discouragement is at hand, do not accept its recommendations or comments such as you can't do that job, you have no education, you are unqualified, just give up; the list goes on and on. You must sow the seeds of "I can, I will, and I must." Remember, "I can do all things through Christ which strengtheneth me" (Philippians 4:13). To God Be The Glory!**

A Ray of Sunshine, A Ray of Hope

The Lord looked down upon Adam standing in the midst of the Garden of Eden. Adam was admiring all of God's creation; he saw the birds and beasts alike, two by two. And how they acted toward one another. Then God said it is not good that man should be alone I will make him a "helpmeet" for him. ***Man was never meant to be alone.*** I believe that God looked into the heart of the man that he created and gave him someone like himself. Eve, the woman was supposed to compliment Adam, the man. She was there to bring companionship and to assist him in maintaining their home (The Garden of Eden). **The institution of marriage has been under attack by evil forces from the beginning of time.** And man can derail that attack by realizing his place in God's creation and claiming it. **Man must realize that marriage is a sacred institution and must never be taken lightly**. Marriage was a new thing; a new God ordained institution and the woman was a different creation. **From the very beginning woman shared a special place in Gods creation of the universe, she was to carry the seed of man and was to be fruitful, multiply and assist the man in subduing the earth**. How great was her task! Apostles, Prophets, Pastors, King's, Queen's, doctors, lawyers, fishermen, brick masons, you name it; was all to be born of a woman from the seed of man. **God himself prepared and used her for his arrival on earth**. **The woman was to be ever careful, because the forces of evil were to bruise her heel (Genesis 3:15-16).** Evil was present in the garden and was set on destroying God's new creation, man and woman. Adam and Eve succumbed to the wiles of the devil and caused their relationship with God to be cut off. Today, man is trying to regain God's trust and ***God is helping him through grace and mercy.*** **The Lord placed a blessing upon the institution called marriage and have given it "honor." Therefore, we are to approach this institution with respect and give it honor before the eyes of God.** How do we get it right! By seeking God first and he will add all things unto us. It is a mistake not to seek God's grace, mercy and guidance before marriage. For he says what two he put together let not man split asunder. **This is a key to marriage, letting God choose your husband or wife for you because when God put you together your marriage will have his blessings and you will succeed in good and bad times.**

This is a key to marriage, letting God choose your husband or wife for you because when God put you together your marriage will have his blessings and you will succeed in good and bad times.

God will protect it, sustain it and help you to keep it holy. Some people say marriage is just a passing fad. Some say it doesn't work anymore. Some say why marry when we can just live together or why marry with so many divorces today, I don't want to be a statistic. **Marriage is not just a passing fad or outdated. Marriage is and still is an honored institution created by God.** If you desire to be married and are ready for it, then pray about it and wait on the Lord. ***He will give you a ray of sunshine and a ray of hope.*** He will give you the desires of your heart. **To God Be the Glory!**

Prayer For Your Marriage

Dear Heavenly Father, who is our provider and the creator of all things, ***write on the tablets of our hearts, a love story that we will follow and cherish all our lives while on our journey to your Kingdom.*** Create a humble, loving and meek spirit in our hearts for each other and those that we cherish so deeply, that we may always discern our needs and desires, and not error in your word; but show love, compassion, joy, peace, understanding, and empathy in our day-to-day lives. ***Father always be that pillar for us to lean on in times of trouble and that our hope will never fade or depart from us.*** Thank you for being the Father who hears and answer our prayers, and for giving us a never-ending fountain of wealth and prosperity. In Jesus name we pray, Amen.

Jesus had compassion on a multitude of followers; he took 5 loaves of bread and 2 fish and fed 5,000 people; (Luke 9:13-17). That same Jesus can take what you have in your relationship and turn it into a wonderful and glorious marriage. To God be the Glory!

Prayer For A Troubled Marriage

Heavenly Father, the Author and Finisher of our Faith; who is the God of Grace, Mercy, Peace and Love. Heavenly Father we come to you in humbleness and meekness of spirit, realizing that we are failing you and your purpose for our marriage. Lord touch our hearts and restore our soul's unto righteousness. Heavenly Father please remove the confusion, the spirit of anger, spirit of fear, the spirit of hurt, spirit of hate, and resentment. ***Join us back together as you joined us from the beginning. Renew that which was lost.*** Lord forgive us for all of our sins and transgressions against you and against one another. Restore and increase the love, peace, compassion and desire that we once cherished so deeply in our hearts for each other. ***Wash our sins away and toss them into the sea of forgetfulness. Strengthen our hearts as to never return to a nature of sin, but to remain Holy before you in all that we do.*** Thank you heavenly Father for your never-ending grace and mercy, in Jesus mighty name we pray, **Amen**.

When Jesus was invited to a wedding, he performed a miracle by turning water into wine; ***he can perform a miracle in your marriage today; just trust in him, believe in him and have faith in him!*** *Expect a healing in your marriage, To God be The Glory!*

Prayer For Seeking Marriage

Dear Heavenly Father, the Creator, Author and Sustainer Of All Things. Father prepare me for the one that you have set aside for me from the beginning of time. Join us together and write the instructions for our marriage on the tablets of our hearts; sealing them until the day of redemption. Instill within our hearts; desire, compassion, love, peace, understanding, faith and obedience that we will always acknowledge toward one another, discerning those things that are pleasing in your eyesight. ***Create an inseparable Bond Of love between us. Give us the strength, faith, knowledge, wisdom and understanding that will sustain us through good and bad times.*** Father ordain it, Bless it and Cover it with your precious blood that we will always acknowledge the Author and Finisher of our Faith, the Lord Jesus Christ. As you bring us together, we receive all that you have for us with Thanksgiving and let us find favor in you. Heavenly Father as you move upon my request, I thank you for your Heavenly Grace and Mercy, in Jesus Mighty Name I pray, Amen.

In the Garden of Eden, the Lord said that it is not good for man to be alone, and that he will make him a "helpmeet" for him. ***God is still in the "helpmeet" making business,*** *let your request be known to him, acknowledge who he is, and receive your blessed marriage with thanksgiving, To God Be The Glory!*

Prayer For Reviving Your Marriage

Heavenly Father, the Creator of all things. To whom we give all praise. Father we come to you in all humbleness and meekness of spirit. We need your protection and blessings in our lives. Father, our marriage is in trouble and we need your heavenly guidance. ***We ask you to restore strength, love, peace and unity back in our home. We are drifting apart day by day and our hearts are failing us. We desire to save our marriage and we know that in you "all things are possible."*** Father; we ask for a Spirit of forgiveness in our hearts for one another for our transgressions are before us. Rebuke every spirit of wickedness against us and break the chains of bondage. Loose the Spirits of love, joy, peace, compassion, unity and endurance in our home. ***Father we welcome your divine presence of Spirit and Truth.*** In our time of need we look to the only one who can redeem what we have lost. Father thank you for your heavenly grace and mercy that is ever before us. Give us peace and understanding that we may restore our love for one another; in the name of "Jesus Christ" we pray, Amen.

Whatever your circumstances may be, **remember God is still in the miracle making business.** *When Leah cried out to him because she felt unloved, he moved upon her situation with miracle, after miracle (Genesis 29:31). Cry out to him for your miracle today! To God Be The Glory!*

Marriage Scriptures

Genesis 2:18

And the Lord God said, it is not good that the man should be alone; I will make him an helpmeet for him.

Genesis 3:6

And when the woman saw that the tree was good for food, and that it was pleasant to the eyes, and a tree to be desired to make one wise, she took of the fruit thereof, and did eat, and gave also unto her husband with her; and he did eat.

Genesis 3:16

Unto the woman he said, I will greatly multiply thy sorrow and thy conception; in sorrow thou shalt bring forth children; and thy desire shall be to thy husband, and he shall rule over thee.

Proverbs 12:4

A virtuous woman is a crown to her husband: but she that maketh ashamed is as rottenness in his bones.

Proverbs 18:22

Whoso findeth a wife findeth a good thing, and obtaineth favour of the Lord.

Proverbs 31:10

Who can find a virtuous woman? For her price is far above rubies.

Hebrews 13:4

Marriage is honorable in all, and the bed undefiled: but whoremongers and adulterers God will judge.

Ephesians. 5:23

For the husband is the head of the wife, even as Christ is the head of the church: and he is the savior of the body.

Ephesians. 5:33

Nevertheless let every one of you in particular so love his wife even as himself; and the wife see that she reverence her husband.

Romans 7:4

Wherefore, my brethren, ye also are become dead to the law by the body of Christ; that ye should be married to another, even to him who is raised from the dead, that we should bring forth fruit unto God.

Luke 1:27

To a virgin espoused to a man whose name was Joseph, of the house of David; and the virgin's name was Mary.

Matthew 1:25

And knew her not till she had brought forth her firstborn son: and he called his name Jesus.

1 Cor. 7:36

But if any man think that he behaveth himself uncomely toward his virgin, if she pass the flower of her age, and need so require, let him do what he will, he sinneth not: let them marry.

1 Cor. 11:11-12

Nevertheless neither is the man without the woman, neither the woman without the man, in the Lord. [12] For as the woman is of the man, even so is the man also by the woman; but all things of God.

2 Cor. 6:14

Be ye not unequally yoked together with unbelievers: for what fellowship hath righteousness with unrighteousness? And what communion hath light with darkness?

1 Cor. 7:15

But if the unbelieving depart, let him depart. A brother or a sister is not under bondage in such cases: but God hath called us to peace.

1 Cor. 11:3

But I would have you know, that the head of every man is Christ; and the head of the woman is the man; and the head of Christ is God.

1 Peter 3:7

Likewise, ye husbands dwell with them according to knowledge, giving honour unto the wife, as unto the weaker vessel, and as being heirs together of the grace of life; that your prayers be not hindered.

Col. 3:18

Wives, submit yourselves unto your own husbands, as it is fit in the Lord.

Matthew 5:31

It hath been said, whosoever shall put away his wife, let him give her a writing of divorcement:

Matthew 5:32

But I say unto you, that whosoever shall put away his wife, saving for the cause of fornication, causeth her to commit adultery: and whosoever shall marry her that is divorced committeth adultery.

Matthew 19:5

And said, for this cause shall a man leave father and mother, and shall cleave to his wife: and they twain shall be one flesh?

Mark 10:29-30

And Jesus answered and said, Verily I say unto you, There is no man that hath left house, or brethren, or sisters, or father, or mother, or wife, or children, or lands, for my sake, and the gospel's, [30] But he shall receive an hundredfold now in this time, houses, and brethren, and sisters, and mothers, and children, and lands, with persecutions; and in the world to come eternal life.

Ephes. 5:28

So ought men to love their wives as their own bodies. He that loveth his wife loveth himself.

Ephes. 5:22

Wives, submit yourselves unto your own husbands, as unto the Lord.

Titus 2:4-5

That they may teach the young women to be sober, to love their husbands, to love their children, [5] To be discreet, chaste, keepers at home, good, obedient to their own husbands, that the word of God be not blasphemed.

Proverbs 21:19

It is better to dwell in the wilderness, than with a contentious and an angry woman.

Proverbs 25:24

It is better to dwell in the corner of the housetop, than with a brawling woman and in a wide house.

Malachi 2:14

Yet ye say, Wherefore? Because the Lord hath been witness between thee and the wife of thy youth, against whom thou hast dealt treacherously: yet is she thy companion, and the wife of thy covenant.

1 Cor. 7:8-9

I say therefore to the unmarried and widows, It is good for them if they abide even as I. [9] But if they cannot contain, let them marry: for it is better to marry than to burn.

Proverbs 5:15

Drink waters out of thine own cistern, and running waters out of thine own well.

1 Cor. 7:2-4

Nevertheless, to avoid fornication, let every man have his own wife, and let every woman have her own husband. [3] Let the

husband render unto the wife due benevolence: and likewise also the wife unto the husband. [4] The wife hath not power of her own body, but the husband: and likewise also the husband hath not power of his own body, but the wife.

1 Tim. 3:2

A bishop then must be blameless, the husband of one wife, vigilant, sober, of good behaviour, given to hospitality, apt to teach;

1 Tim. 3:12

Let the deacons be the husbands of one wife, ruling their children and their own houses well.

Eccles. 9:9

Live joyfully with the wife whom thou lovest all the days of the life of thy vanity, which he hath given thee under the sun, all the days of thy vanity: for that is thy portion in this life, and in thy labour which thou takest under the sun.

Proverbs 19:13

A foolish son is the calamity of his father: and the contentions of a wife are a continual dropping.

Proverbs 19:14

House and riches are the inheritance of fathers and a prudent wife is from the Lord.

Eccles. 7:9

Be not hasty in thy spirit to be angry: for anger resteth in the bosom of fools.

Proverbs 15:1

A soft answer turneth away wrath: but grievous words stir up anger.

Eccles. 3:1

To every thing there is a season, and a time to every purpose under the heaven:

Ephes. 4:26-27

Be ye angry, and sin not: let not the sun go down upon your wrath: [27] Neither give place to the devil.

Matthew 6:23

But if thine eye be evil, thy whole body shall be full of darkness. If therefore the light that is in thee be darkness, how great is that darkness!

James 1:14

But every man is tempted, when he is drawn away of his own lust, and enticed.

Genesis 4:26

And to Seth, to him also there was born a son; and he called his name Enos: then began men to call upon the name of the Lord.

Ephes. 5:25-26

Husbands, love your wives, even as Christ also loved the church, and gave himself for it; [26] That he might sanctify and cleanse it with the washing of water by the word,

Proverbs 22:1

A good name is rather to be chosen than great riches, and loving favour rather than silver and gold.

Genesis 2:24

Therefore shall a man leave his father and his mother, and shall cleave unto his wife: and they shall be one flesh.

Matthew 19:6

Wherefore they are no more twain, but one flesh. What therefore God hath joined together, let not man put asunder.

Matthew 5:27

Ye have heard that it was said by them of old time, Thou shalt not commit adultery:

1 Tim. 5:8

But if any provide not for his own, and specially for those of his own house, he hath denied the faith, and is worse than an infidel.

2 Peter 2:22

But it is happened unto them according to the true proverb, The dog is turned to his own vomit again; and the sow that was washed to her wallowing in the mire.

1 Cor. 6:8-10

Nay, ye do wrong, and defraud, and that your brethren. [9] Know ye not that the unrighteous shall not inherit the kingdom of God? Be not deceived: neither fornicators, nor idolaters, nor adulterers, nor effeminate, nor abusers of themselves with mankind, [10] Nor thieves, nor covetous, nor drunkards, nor revilers, nor extortioners, shall inherit the kingdom of God.

Final Note...

Marriage can be greatly rewarding, but it must be the right mix of heart, soul and spirit. You must be on one accord. Love must be the pure fuel that serves as a catalyst to keep the fires of passion and desire burning. Midnight oil should be burning because of intimate desire, not arguing or complaining about each other's shortcomings. **Every opportunity should be to express love for each other, both inwardly and outwardly.** Consider your spouse first, provide for her comfort and your comfort will follow. **Keep God in your lives and welcome his presence daily**. Remember, **the words "I Love You" can warm the coldest of hearts. To God be the Glory!**